WE GON' BE ALRIGHT

WE GON' BE ALRIGHT

NOTES ON RACE AND RESEGREGATION

Jeff Chang

PICADOR

New York

picadorusa.com • picadorbookroom.tumblr.com
twitter.com/picadorusa • facebook.com/picadorusa

Picador® is a U.S. registered trademark and is used by Macmillan Publishing Group, LLC, under license from Pan Books Limited.

For book club information, please visit facebook.com /picadorbookclub or e-mail marketing@picadorusa.com.

Cover art courtesy of Damon Davis, from the "All Hands On Deck" poster series. 2015. allhandsondeckproject.org/

The author gratefully acknowledges permission to republish lyrics from "I Can't Breathe" by Luke Nephew of the Peace Poets.

Visit Jeff Chang online at: jeffchang.net • bealright.net • twitter.com/zentronix • facebook.com/jeffchangwriter

The Library of Congress Cataloging-in-Publication Data is available upon request.

ISBN 978-0-312-42948-5 (trade paperback)
ISBN 978-1-250-11479-2 (e-book)

Our books may be purchased in bulk for promotional, educational, or business use. Please contact your local bookseller or the Macmillan Corporate and Premium Sales Department at 1-800-221-7945, extension 5442, or by e-mail at MacmillanSpecialMarkets@macmillan.com.

First Edition: September 2016

10   9   8

In appreciation of all the young people
who would not bow down

. . . And all of this for you is fuel
like September *kiawe*.
You vow to write so hard
the paper burns

CONTENTS

WE GON' BE ALRIGHT

INTRODUCTION

THE CRISIS CYCLE

We are living in serious times. Since 2012, the names of the fallen—Trayvon Martin, Michael Brown, Tamir Rice, Freddie Gray, Sandra Bland, Laquan McDonald, the list never seems to cease—have catalyzed collective outrage and grief. In the waning years of a Black presidency, we saw a proliferation of images of Black people killed in the streets and the rise of a national justice movement to affirm that Black lives matter.

Young people who grew up exemplars of post-1965 American diversity while attending schools that were dramatically resegregating have taken to the streets and the university quads to march against their own invisibility and demand a renewed attention to questions of equity.

And even the machines of our culture industries, which for the past twenty years have tried to assure us that our rainbow nation is indeed a happy one, have found their gears ground down by popular protests led by people of color against their lack of access, representation, and power.

In *Who We Be*, I wrote about visual culture and what I called the paradox of the "post-racial" moment—that while our images depict a nation moving toward desegregation, our indices reveal growing resegregation and inequity. The book was published a month before the announcement of the non-indictment of officer Darren Wilson in Ferguson, Missouri. Since then, the idea that there had ever been a post-racial moment has come to seem naive, even desperately so.

Once the embodiment of hope, Obama leaves office publicly regretting his inability to reconcile the country's polarization. At the same time, Donald Trump focuses the anxieties loosed by white vulnerability—an inchoate, inescapable sense that the social and economic present and future of whites will only get worse—onto the bodies of migrants, Muslims, Blacks, women, and all those others who do not deserve the gift of America. Like climate change, the culture wars seem to have become an enduring feature of our daily lives, the permanent fog of a country that repeats the spectacle of fire in every generation.

Polls show that more Americans are concerned about race relations now than at any time since 1992, the year of the Los Angeles riots. The previous peak had come in 1965—the year of the Voting Rights Act, the Immigration and Nationality Act, the apex of the civil rights movement, the year of the last national consensus for racial justice.

1965 was also the year of Malcolm X's assassination and the Watts riots. It was the beginning of the post–civil rights era, an era that has been defined by a vital culture reshaped under demographic change but a politics mobilized around racial backlash. That historic arc—of an explosion of cultural expression that moved us forward toward mutual recognition amidst a cascade of regressive policies, laws, and political maneuvers that pushed us backward toward inequality and resegregation—was my focus in *Who We Be*. Over the past two years, it seems even clearer that we as a nation are caught in a bad loop of history—from 1965 to 1992 to right now.

Race makes itself known in crisis, in the singular event that captures a larger pattern of abuse and pain. We react to crisis with a flurry of words and, sometimes, actions. In turn, the reaction sparks its own backlash of outrage, justification, and denial. The cycle turns next toward exhaustion, complacency, and paralysis. And before long, we find ourselves back in crisis.

Racism is not merely about individual chauvinism, prejudice, or bigotry. Ruth Gilmore reminds us that it is about the ways different groups are "vulnerable to premature death," whether at the hands of the state or the structures that kill.[1]

We know now that implicit bias, stereotype threat, and the empathy gap are real things. People harbor subconscious biases that are hard to root out but can be unlearned. Social psychologist Jennifer Eberhardt, for example, has argued that training police to see the way in which people subconsciously associate criminality with Black faces can reduce rates of racial profiling.

But the social structures that create premature death do not harm only those individuals who have the misfortune to come into contact with bigots or quick-trigger authorities who have not yet learned how to see. They also prevent people from getting adequate food, shelter, and housing. They limit physical, economic, and social mobility. They refuse to let us all be free. Over time, these structures have proven extraordinarily adaptable.

Inequity and injustice are not abstract things. They impact real people and real lives. In terms of poverty, annual income, wealth, health, housing, schooling, and incarceration, persistent gaps separate whites from Black,

Latino, Southeast Asian, Pacific Islander, and American Indian populations.[2] And in the specific case of premature death—defined by the Centers for Disease Control and Prevention as death among persons under the age of seventy-five—the death rate of Blacks is over 50 percent higher than that of whites, and higher than that of all other major ethnic groups, except for some American Indian cohorts.

Only a small part of this statistic is attributable to homicide and that favorite digression of conservative pundits, "Black-on-Black violence." In fact, most of the reasons have to do with large disparities in access to quality food and regular and preventative health care, and with diseases such as cancer, stroke, and HIV. A shockingly large portion is the result of an African American infant mortality rate that is more than double that of white Americans, triple that of Swiss citizens, and five times that of Japanese citizens.[3] Racism kills.

Extrajudicial police shootings have been the organizing spark of the Movement for Black Lives. But the facts of inequality and death hang over us all like a toxic haze. In the United States, segregation and resegregation happen through the disappearing of the signs of inequality. Whether through white flight, the optics of diversity, or metaphorical and actual wall building, the privileged spare themselves the sight of disparity, and foreclose the possibility of empathy and transformation.

Now this haze has blown into white America as well. More white U.S. women and men in their forties and fifties—particularly those with lower levels of educational attainment—are dying prematurely. This reversal of fortune for middle-aged whites is unprecedented in American history and unique among the wealthy nations. When examining the causes, researchers Anne Case and Angus Deaton found significant rises in painkiller abuse, liver disease, suicides, and drug overdoses. "Future financial insecurity may weigh more heavily on U.S. workers," they wrote, calling middle-aged whites a "'lost generation' whose future is less bright than those who preceded them."[4] At the height of the Reagan-Bush era the writer Barbara Ehrenreich named this condition: whites, whose once solid destinies were melting into air, harbor a deep "fear of falling." That tumble is now all too real.

A turn in fortune should move us toward empathy and solidarity. When a natural disaster tears apart a village, the human tendency is for one neighbor to help another, regardless of whatever feelings they may have had for one another before the catastrophe. But we live in a time when merchants of division draw us away from mutuality and toward the undoing of democracy itself.

David Graeber proposes that their demagoguery is not so different from schoolyard bullying, which is "a kind of elementary structure of human domination."[5] Trump, the silver spoon–fed child who, as a second grader, punched his music teacher in the eye, aspired "to be the toughest kid in the neighborhood."[6] He described himself as "very well liked . . . the kid that others followed."[7] Bullies, Graeber argues, don't usually lack self-esteem. They do not see themselves as outcasts but as heroes.

Dylann Storm Roof, the young man who murdered nine Black parishioners in a prayer meeting in Charleston, South Carolina, in the hope of starting a race war, wrote that he "was not raised in a racist home or environment." He had Black friends, or at least acquaintances. One who had known him from childhood said, "He wasn't like: 'When I grow up I am going to show all these kids.'" Instead, Roof wanted to lead by example.

The bully needs an audience to enable his act. "When researchers question children on why they do not intervene [to protect the bullied], a minority say they felt the victim got what he or she deserved," Graeber writes, "but the majority say they didn't like what happened, and certainly didn't much like the bully, but decided that getting involved might mean ending up on the receiving end of the same treatment—and that would only make things worse."[8]

Culture-war extremists do two things. They water the seed of insecurity into a weed of hate. They do so by seizing on white fears of the future, conflating economic insecurity and looming demographic eclipse. The first is as tangible as monthly bills, specific, looming, and real; the second is as subrational and inarticulate as seeing Taylor Swift perform with Kendrick Lamar.

Dylann Storm Roof wrote in his conflicted, contradictory manifesto, "Why should we have to flee the cities we created for the security of the suburbs? Why are the suburbs secure in the first place? Because they are White . . . Who is fighting for these White people forced by economic circumstances to live among negroes? No one, but someone has to." Roof, like other extremists, believed in the restoration of white power. The main way Roof departed from the rest was in his insistence that the restoration be violently begun and maintained. He took the metaphor of war seriously.

But even for those who say they don't like the bullying and don't like the bully, the culture wars allow them cover to do nothing. Demagogues evoke restorationist dream-

ing, a deeply imagined past of order and tranquility. Re-
actionaries do not even need to sustain the belief or the
anger of the fearful; they need only the silence and the
complicity of the masses. In this way, from Wallace and
Nixon to Palin and Trump, the energies of anxious whites
have been diverted from class uprising toward racial division.

The culture wars continue through justificatory innocence and willed inaction. They *allow* the structures that
produce inequality and segregation to persist. They even
generate the ideas that adapt those structures to better en-
force racialized exclusion.

Before the 1980s, it was mostly Marxists who used the
term "politically correct" to mock other Marxists. Since
then, charging someone else with political correctness
has become the first line of defense for racists, one of the
best ways to shut down any discussion about inequity.
That silencing isolates the most marginalized communities, and demobilizes white communities. Resegregation
grows not from white ignorance, but from white refusal
and denial. And so a half century after the peak of the
civil rights movement, the nation has moved again into
crisis.

One need not be a pessimist to see the bad loop of
history we are caught within—crisis, reaction, backlash,
complacency, crisis. There are fires. There are calls for action. There is then a bullying politics of fear. If most
Americans recoil from the kind of excessive, gleeful, cynical bigotry someone like the billionaire Donald Trump
proffers, they are yet demobilized to the point of denial
("there is no problem") or justification ("there is a problem but I can't solve it"). And then we find ourselves in
another crisis.

In *We Gon' Be Alright*, I look at some of the ways in which we have slid back toward segregation. To be sure, there has never been a time when we did not live separately. In 2014, more than 300 school districts across the country were still involved in active desegregation orders dating to the civil rights era.[9] At the same time, even as we have come to mostly celebrate "diversity," resegregation is happening all around us: in our neighborhoods and schools, our colleges and universities, even in the culture. The culture wars have obscured and exacerbated these facts. Worse, they have left us without a common understanding or language that might help us to end them.

What I hope to show in this book is how inequality and segregation impact us all. Our destinies are interconnected, but not all of us have the best vantage point to see our way out of the fog of the culture wars. Some of us still can't even see each other fully. But those who suffer the most have the most to teach the entire nation about how to move away from it all, if we choose to listen and act.

What today's activists, organizers, and artists are giving us are new ways to see our past and our present. Even more, they are giving us the directive to address inequality and inequity now—to make it clear that if we do not do so, we will continue to be drawn back into the bad cycle, just as we were after 1965, and after 1992. Right now we have the opportunity to get it right. Our shared future depends upon it.

IS DIVERSITY FOR WHITE PEOPLE?

ON FEARMONGERING, PICTURE TAKING, AND AVOIDANCE

In December 2015, Donald Trump held a noon rally at an airport hangar in Mesa, Arizona, a largely white suburb in the Phoenix sprawl that had been the spawning ground for the viciously anti-immigrant law S.B. 1070.

Maricopa County Sheriff Joe Arpaio, taking a break from defending himself from Department of Justice charges that he had violated a federal court order against racial profiling, kept the stage warm. "You're the patriots," he told the audience. They were the ones worth protecting— with Arpaio's men and guns and jails, and with Trump's grand border wall. The sheriff continued, "One thing about him, I think he'll really do what he says. I really do." The placards that had been distributed read, "The Silent Majority Stands with Trump." In the state of Barry Goldwater, Trump was putting on a display of firepower and nostalgia.

Trump made his grand entrance. His Boeing 757, emblazoned with his name in bold on the side, rolled to a stop in front of the hangar and a crowd of several thousand. From the top of the gangway he waved, then descended the stairs to Twisted Sister's mid-eighties hair-metal hit "We're Not Gonna Take It."

First, he did a live interview with Bill O'Reilly. Large American and Arizonan flags and the enormous crowd served as his backdrop. O'Reilly began questioning Trump almost apologetically, as if recognizing that he had wandered onto hostile turf. When Trump dissed Fox News for "saying untrue things about me" and blustered that he would do "pretty severe stuff" to stop terrorism, the crowd roared.

O'Reilly asked, "Are you gonna tell me tonight on this program that you don't say stuff just to get at the emotion of the voter? I know you do."

"I'm telling you right now that I don't. I do the right thing. I bring up subjects that are important. I bring up illegal immigration," Trump said. "And if I didn't bring it up you wouldn't even be talking about illegal immigration." The crowd started chanting his name.

O'Reilly persisted. "You don't do this to whip up the base, whip up your crowd?"

"I don't, I don't," Trump said. "I say what's right, I say what's on my mind, and that's what's happening."

After the interview he stepped up to the podium to deliver a long speech in his churlish, digressive style, dispensing ample insults to his many enemies. "Somebody said, 'Oh, Trump's a great entertainer.' That's a lot of bullshit, I'll tell you," he said. "We have a message, we have a message, and the message is we don't want to let other people take advantage of us."[1]

In his best seller *The Art of the Deal*, Trump's advice was to "know your market" and "use your leverage." Trump knew his market. He understood the inchoate white anger cohering in the country well ahead of Republican party leaders and media elites. "Leverage," Trump wrote, "is having something the other guy wants. Or better yet, needs. Or best of all, simply can't do without."[2]

In 2011, Obama, who had become for disaffected whites

the image of all fears, provided Trump with leverage. Trump made himself the public face of the bizarre Birther movement, which held that Barack Obama had not been born in the United States. In naming Obama an "illegal alien," conspiracists could attach fantastical narratives to Obama: Chicago criminal corruption, Muslim takeovers, Mexican drug-dealer invasions.

Despite the fact that Obama had already released a short-form certification of live birth, Trump sent investigators to Hawai'i to uncover what he called "one of the greatest cons in the history of politics and beyond." Obama responded by releasing a long-form version of his birth certificate. Outplayed, Trump still declared victory, saying, "I am so proud of myself because I've accomplished something that nobody else was able to accomplish." He had forced the first Black president to become the first standing president in history forced to defend the legitimacy of his birthright. And he had captured the attention and the affection of frustrated white voters. But at that moment Trump retreated, quietly walking away from a presidential bid. The time had not yet come.

By 2015, though, it had. Whites undone by skyrocketing economic inequality, distrustful of big business and media, ignored by elites—the middle and working class, whose fears of falling were being realized—needed someone to vocalize their anger and anxiety. Trump found ready scapegoats. He called Mexican immigrants "criminals" and "rapists," warned that "Islam hates us," and accused China of "waging economic war against us." He pandered to whites' fragility, played on their glory-days nostalgia. His ham-fisted "Make America Great Again" slogan—so prosaic and dull next to Reagan's "Morning in America"—seemed designed for bro-style fist-pumping, not gauzy restorationist dreaming. As one supporter put it: "Trump is a winner and I'm sick of losing."[3]

His candidacy wreaked havoc on the Republican primaries. The party had become calcified with rules, protocols, etiquette. Trump descended from the air and the airwaves to talk shit. He entertained. He created the vibe that he was a billionaire you could share a hot dog and a can of Coors with, even though deep down you knew he never would. You went to Trump; he never came to you. It created a desire, a longing. And so even as Trump kept an army of fact-checkers well employed—fully 77 percent of the Trump statements that PolitiFact had investigated were rated "Mostly False," "False," or "Pants on Fire!"— the last thing his supporters cared about was the facts. They had feelings, and no one else understood them like Trump did.

One supporter told Ryan Lizza of the *New Yorker*, "The birth certificate stuff, I loved. I watched all the YouTube videos on it, and what he was saying made sense." She added, "I'm dead set [on voting for him] unless I find out something down the line. But I'm not going to believe what the media tells me. I have to hear it from him. The media does not persuade me one bit."[4]

For Trump diehards in a time of danger and disjunction, the media's job was not to challenge, but to affirm. So when demonstrators poured into the streets to protest police killings of Blacks, the media was supposed to confirm for them that those chaos makers were actually supporting the killing of cops, that somehow the Movement for Black Lives was a Black version of the Ku Klux Klan. And some pundits—Hannity, the same O'Reilly who confronted Trump—dutifully filled this role.[5] In their telling, "Black lives matter" was not a call to end state violence against Blacks—and in that way, to end state violence against all—it was evidence of hatred against whites, a premonition of racial apocalypse.

White liberal media recoiled. To them, Trump supporters were unseemly, irrational, embarrassing. They looked for an explanation and, by the end of 2015, found it in Angus Deaton and Anne Case's scholarship on the rising rates of white suicide, drug overdose, and premature death. Deaton and Case had helped white liberal media rediscover the steeply declining white middle and working class.

It was not a little ironic that the Movement for Black Lives had opened up a fresh discussion about white mortality. When the conversation in this country is about race, all too often it leads back to whiteness. But as Alicia Garza, one of the founders of Black Lives Matter, has written, "When Black people get free, everyone gets free."[6] Inequality impacts us unequally. The truth is that we cannot address it without starting from the bottom. But fear is the enemy of truth and division the master key of demagogues. Democracy was just another hustle for Trump, one that he could play best in the scrum of the popular culture, where his skill with the levers of the media was unparalleled. Race would be his shortcut to attention and conversion, and he could figure out the details of the game later.

What Trump understood best was how banal facts could be marshaled to unleash hysterical exigency. After the breakthrough civil rights victories of the early 1960s, it was commonplace to note that each generation was the most diverse in the nation's history. Objectively, the data projected that whites would drop below 50 percent of the national population within a generation. But to Trump voters, coastal pundits and paid experts did not understand what that really meant. Change meant erasure.

Racial apocalypse is the recurring white American narrative in which the civilizers, the chosen people meant to fulfill their destiny, are overrun by the savages, the barbarians who embody chaos and ruin. It's in the stories told about the Alamo, General Custer, Reconstruction, the sixties. It's even there in the fixation on the Civil War, Lincoln's life and assassination, and the common disappearance of slavery from that story. The racial apocalypse is part of the DNA of American pop culture—Buffalo Bill Cody's cowboys-and-Indians show, D. W. Griffith's *The Birth of a Nation*—but instead of bloodshed and death, we got happy endings. The end of whiteness is one of the oldest, most common stories Americans tell to scare ourselves (even though we don't all scare equally).

So in the Southern heat of 2009, Tea Party activists appeared under Confederate flags bearing signs that read, "Bring Back 'We the People.'" Trump's Birther campaign followed. And by 2015, Trump voters were flipping off everyone who argued that diversity was inevitable—the grabby minorities, their liberal-media apologists, the corrupt Republican party elite—retorting, "Not over me."

When Black Lives Matter and DREAM activists began to demonstrate at Trump rallies, violence erupted. In Birmingham, Alabama, Trump supporters tackled, punched, and kicked a Black protester. In Las Vegas, another Black protester was dragged out of a Trump rally as supporters shouted, "Kick his ass," "Light the motherfucker on fire," "*Sieg Heil*," and "He's a Muslim guy!" Tensions climaxed in Chicago, as hundreds of demonstrators and supporters clashed in the University of Illinois arena, forcing Trump to cancel his rally at the last minute.

After two brothers in Boston attacked a homeless Latino man with a pipe and then pissed on him, shouting, "Donald Trump was right, all these illegals need to be deported," Trump tweeted that he "would never condone violence." But he also said, "I will say, the people that are following me are passionate. They love this country, they want this country to be great again."[7] At times, he seemed delighted by the aggressive physicality of his supporters. After demonstrators interrupted his Vegas rally, he told supporters, "We should have been doing what they're doing for the last seven years because what's happening to our country is a disgrace."[8] No one had any doubt about whom Trump meant when he said "we," "they," and "our."

A few days later, as security at an Oklahoma City rally surrounded a young protester, Trump said, "You see, in the good old days, law enforcement acted a lot quicker than this. But today everyone is so politically correct. Our country is going to hell—we're being politically correct."

He concluded, "We are really becoming a frightened country, and it's very, very sad."

The Picture of Diversity

On an April morning before the New York primary, a group calling itself the National Diversity Coalition for Trump called media to an event at Trump Tower. They intended to demonstrate that their man had broad support from communities of color.

The event did not go well. Organizers—including *The Apprentice* star Omarosa Manigault, a gaggle of Black pastors, as well as members of Arab Americans for Trump, Muslim Americans for Trump, and Hispanic Patriots for Trump—did not know when Trump would speak. When he did arrive, he talked for less than five minutes, never addressed his campaign's diversity efforts, then disappeared back into the elevator. "What was billed as a press conference seemed more of a photo op and dash," NBC News's Ali Vitali wrote.[9] The Diversity Coalition stood around wondering if the meeting they hoped to have with Trump was still happening.

This tale of Trump's sad little Coalition tells us as much about the story of diversity now as Trump's race-baiting and countenancing of violence do. It's about the ways diversity has been exploited and rendered meaningless in a time when change is thought of in terms of numbers, appraisals, and images.

In early 2000, the University of Wisconsin began preparing its admissions application to send out to prospective undergrads. The proposed cover featured a photo of its student body at a home football game cheering on their team. There was only one problem, which the African American vice chancellor quickly pointed out to the admissions director: the photo featured only white students.

The staff spent the summer looking for photos that might show happy students in Badger red being diverse together. (At the time, the university was 90 percent white.) They could not find one they deemed suitable. Instead the staff found a photo of a broadly smiling Black male student, and cut-and-pasted his head into the picture behind two exuberant white women. Over 100,000 applications were printed and sent out.[10]

One day, that Black student walked into the admissions office. His name was Diallo Shabazz and he was known on campus as an excellent scholar who worked under the vice chancellor to tutor inner-city teens of color in precollege summer programs. An admissions counselor stopped him to tell him he was on the cover of the application. Shabazz stared at the photo. He had never been to a football game.

Soon the story had become a minor national controversy. Some argued that the doctored photo represented the "intellectual dishonesty of racial-preference programs," as if the floating signifier of Shabazz's digitized head were somehow a threat to American meritocracy. But many more wondered about the university's institutional goals. Whom was the image meant to attract? Students of color, who had long been underrepresented at the University of Wisconsin? Or white students and parents who could be assured that the campus was indeed elite and non-racist? Was diversity for everybody, for people of color, or just for white people?

In the coming decade, urban neighborhoods would be marketed for their "diversity," corporations and colleges would appoint chief diversity officers and increase their holdings of assets directed at "diverse demographics," while pushing ads—sometimes also doctored—that featured happy, diverse consumers. The college-admissions industrial complex began using diversity in its rankings criteria, even as the courts continued to chip away at and voters dismantled the affirmative action programs that many whites disliked.

During the 1980s, campuses like the University of California at Berkeley and the University of Michigan tied together notions of diversity and excellence. At the time the link was startling for some. But by the turn of the millennium, diversity and excellence—or perhaps, more specifically, the appearance of each—were bound together. The appearance of diversity signaled excellence, and the appearance of excellence signaled diversity.

The scholar Nancy Leong named this new arrangement "racial capitalism." She argued that white individuals and predominantly white institutions derived "social or economic value from associating with individuals with nonwhite racial identities." She wrote that "in a society preoccupied with diversity, nonwhiteness is a valued commodity. And where that society is founded on capitalism, it is unsurprising that the commodity of nonwhiteness is exploited for its market value."[11]

Remember the strange case of Rachel Dolezal, the woman who was born white, sued Howard University for discriminating against her in part because she was white, but then went on to lead the Spokane NAACP as a "Black-identifying" woman?[12] Or perhaps the story of Michael Derrick Hudson, a white poet who wrote under the name of a high school classmate, Yi-Fen Chou, in an attempt to have his writing recognized by diversity-minded judges? Both seemed extreme examples of racial capitalism—whites who valued diversity so much that they decided to fake it.

Anna Holmes writes that the value of diversity extends to "moral credibility," an idea that captures individualized dimensions of white fragility and points directly to the ethics of white agency. In Dolezal's case, what began as fakery developed into an ultimately failed act of passing, with its complicated, combustible brew of identification, appropriation, and displacement. Hudson, for his part, believed that masking himself in diversity might confer on him relevance and gravitas. If Dolezal felt responsibility for her adopted siblings and her biracial children, Hudson understood that diversity could really be just about optics. These were stories—to borrow the title of Eric Lott's famous book on blackface minstrelsy—of love and theft.

When Shabazz and other Black students at the University of Wisconsin learned of the Photoshop fiasco, they were bemused and befuddled. "The admissions department that we've been talking about, I believe, was on the fourth floor, and the multicultural center was on the second floor of the same building," Shabazz recalled later to National Public Radio. "So you didn't need to create false diversity in the picture—all you really needed to do was go downstairs."[13] Or upstairs. The Black Student Union's president, Jana Thompson, told reporters that their office was one floor up from the admissions department, and that she could have given them photos if they had asked.

The original photo of Shabazz featured him sitting among a crowd of white students. He was the focus of the photo, and all the white faces in the frame were turned away or cut off. It makes one wonder: Couldn't university administrators have deployed this picture in their application materials? Or did they think it more suitable to paste a Black face into a photo in which whites were centered? What was the minimum threshold of color necessary for an acceptable presentation of diversity? The University of Wisconsin remained an institution whose student body was only 2 percent Black. Diversity imparted value, and it was still a much lower standard than equity.

Diallo Shabazz sued the University of Wisconsin. Not for an apology, but for what he called a "budgetary apology"—reparations, if you will. And he won. The university earmarked $10 million for the recruitment of students of color and the implementation of diversity initiatives. Lisa Wade, one of Shabazz's teachers, wrote the coda: "The irony in the whole thing is that UW requested photos of Shabazz shaking administrators' hands in reconciliation (i.e., photographic proof that everything was just fine)."[14] In the digital stream of images flowing from the story, administrators hoped the last would be one that restored the impression of the University of Wisconsin as an excellent, diverse school.

More Than Freedom

The official use of the word "diversity" reveals a story of compromise and redirection. The word itself was a semi-obscure one, favored by an esoteric group of ecologists and cultural equity activists, until Justice Lewis Powell Jr. plucked it out to use in his opinion in the 1978 *Regents of the University of California v. Bakke* case. For better and for worse, Powell profoundly changed how we talk about race in America. Because of that case, "diversity" has been inextricably entwined with another weird phrase: "affirmative action."

For a long time, the debate over affirmative action was a proxy for discussing race and inequality. It was a way to talk about debt and reparations, guilt and transformation, without ever using those words. With each succeeding Supreme Court case, it seems that philosophy, pragmatism, and policy receive diminishing returns.

As Terry H. Anderson writes in his history *The Pursuit of Fairness*, the word "affirmative" and the word "action" may have first appeared together in the 1935 Wagner Act, also known as the National Labor Relations Act, the law that guaranteed collective bargaining rights for private-sector laborers. The term was associated with a different kind of inequality back then, as a remedy for workers who had been discriminated against—offending employers were required to take "affirmative action" to restore the salary or position the employee would otherwise have had.[15] The term did not explicitly speak to racial discrimination. It created more broadly the notion of a class in need of protection for whom equity needed to be restored or achieved. Anderson and other historians, notably Ira Katznelson, have argued that government efforts—such as New Deal policies around housing, welfare, Social Security, Medicaid, and labor, or the postwar G.I. Bill—were effectively affirmative action programs for protected classes composed predominantly of whites.[16]

By the 1960s, during a period of an emerging civil rights consensus, African Americans and other underrepresented minorities who had suffered discrimination were finally deemed worthy of consideration as a protected class. Through a series of executive orders issued first by President Kennedy and then by President Johnson, and later in the 1964 Civil Rights Act (which enjoyed the support of 70 percent of the country), the government response to racial justice movements took shape, first through a colorblind principle of nondiscrimination and then in the use of affirmative action as a colorconscious weapon to reverse racial discrimination and segregation.[17]

In a June 4, 1965, commencement speech at Howard University, President Johnson articulated the shift:

> But freedom is not enough. You do not wipe away the scars of centuries by saying: "Now you are free to go

where you want, and do as you desire, and choose the leaders you please."

You do not take a person who, for years, has been hobbled by chains and liberate him, bring him up to the starting line of a race and then say, "You are free to compete with all the others," and still justly believe that you have been completely fair.

Thus it is not enough just to open the gates of opportunity. All our citizens must have the ability to walk through those gates.

This is the next and the more profound stage of the battle for civil rights. We seek not just freedom but opportunity. We seek not just legal equity but human ability, not just equality as a right and a theory but equality as a fact and equality as a result.

For the task is to give 20 million Negroes the same chance as every other American to learn and grow, to work and share in society, to develop their abilities—physical, mental and spiritual—and to pursue their individual happiness.[18]

Beginning in the early 1960s, elite universities—including Michigan, Harvard, Cornell, and UCLA, all historically white institutions whose student-of-color populations were negligibly small—adopted affirmative action programs.[19] At many of these campuses, students of color demanded proportional representation, but administrators opted for more gradualist programs, taking on the governmental language of analysis, goals, and timetables.[20]

Over the next three decades, educational, governmental, and corporate institutions across the country developed and expanded affirmative action plans to open doors for Blacks and other minorities. The broad-based civil rights movement became a battle waged largely by politicians, lawyers, administrators, and academics focused on claims of rights and opportunity.

In 1978, the *Bakke* decision crystallized debates that had been raging since the outset of affirmative action. And it did so in the context of California, a key demographic forerunner of the rest of the nation.

At the time, California's population was over 25 percent nonwhite. Plaintiff Allan Bakke wanted to attend the University of California at Davis medical program, which reserved sixteen of its one hundred slots annually for disadvantaged students via a special admissions program. Twice, the med school rejected Bakke. The California Supreme Court ruled six to one that the special admissions program was a quota system and was unconstitutional. It also held that any consideration of race in admissions was unconstitutional.

In a 1977 op-ed titled "Reparation, American Style," the *New York Times* framed the question before the court like so: "Should we reduce opportunity for whites— somewhat—so as to accelerate opportunity for some blacks and other victims of pervasive discrimination?"[21] To supporters of affirmative action, Bakke's victory denied the history of racial discrimination and segregation, the fact of underrepresentation, and preserved white entitlement. But to opponents, Bakke's case defined "reverse racism" against whites.

The U.S. Supreme Court split down the middle. Four justices—Chief Justice Burger, along with Justices Stevens, Rehnquist, and Stewart—agreed with the California Supreme Court. Four—Brennan, White, Marshall, and Blackmun—supported the affirmative action program.

In order to secure a majority, Justice Lewis Powell Jr. proposed to cut the baby in half, finding the special admissions program unconstitutional but allowing that the university—and, in turn, the government—had a compelling interest in seeking diversity.

Powell first argued that fidelity to colorblindness all but denied any consideration of previous discrimination based on race. "Racial and ethnic distinctions of any sort are inherently suspect and thus call for the most exacting judicial examination," he wrote. But race, along with other kinds of factors—such as geography or "cultural disadvantage"—enriched the educational experience for all. Such "plus factors" together constituted "genuine diversity."

Powell drew extensively—and quite unironically—on Harvard's admissions plan, writing:

> The belief that diversity adds an essential ingredient to the educational process has long been a tenet of Harvard College admissions. Fifteen or twenty years ago, however, diversity meant students from California, New York, and Massachusetts; city dwellers and farm boys; violinists, painters and football players; biologists, historians and classicists; potential stockbrokers, academics and politicians. *The result was that very few ethnic or racial minorities attended Harvard College.* In recent years Harvard College has expanded the concept of diversity to include students from disadvantaged economic, racial and ethnic groups. Harvard College now recruits not only Californians or Louisianans but also blacks and Chicanos and other minority students. Contemporary conditions in the United States mean that if Harvard

College is to continue to offer a first-rate education to its students, minority representation in the under-graduate body cannot be ignored by the Committee on Admissions.[22]

Powell had disappeared racial exclusion from the history of higher education, and redirected discussion of affirmative action into a decontextualized present. He radically flattened difference. *You're a farm boy. You're a violinist. You're a Louisianan. You're Black. You're Chicano.* He had affirmed that diversity really was for white people.

By contrast, Justice Blackmun noted that only 2 percent of doctors in the country were of color, and wondered why, of all admissions preferences, the one remedying racial discrimination should be singled out for condemnation. He added, "I suspect it would be impossible to arrange an affirmative-action program in a racially neutral way and have it successful. To ask that this be so is to demand the impossible."

Justice Thurgood Marshall was even more direct. "It is more than a little ironic that, after several hundred years of class-based discrimination against Negroes, the Court is unwilling to hold that a class-based remedy for that discrimination is permissible." But with Powell's decision, diversity displaced equity as the only viable defense of programs meant to address underrepresentation.

In 1979, just after the Bakke case was decided, 67 percent of whites supported affirmative action.[23] But Powell had opened the door for opponents to attack the program as harmful to whites. To achieve diversity, he seemed to argue, you didn't need quotas, you just needed optics. Powell's diversity rationale countenanced a Noah's

Ark approach—add two of each to the Ark to escape the rising floodwaters. The climate-change analogy feels apt: the problem of racial segregation and exclusion had been wholly man-made. Powell's solution did not address the problem so much as redirect the forces around it. Diversity was the rainbow sign. After the flood, the fire next time.

The Reagan administration, no friends of civil rights, argued that affirmative action unfairly limited opportunities for whites. And in the coming years, opponents of affirmative action, whether conservative or liberal, broadened their attack on all manner of attempts to achieve racial and cultural equity—in jobs, government contracts, fair housing, bank loans, executive leadership, even university canons and desegregated schools—as antiwhite.

Those who study segregation now mark 1989 as the peak year of public school desegregation. That year, in *City of Richmond v. J. A. Croson Company*, Justice Sandra Day O'Connor reiterated that the court was loathe to weigh claims of past discrimination: "The dream of a Nation of equal citizens in a society where race is irrelevant to personal opportunity and achievement would be lost in a mosaic of shifting preferences based on inherently unmeasurable claims of past wrongs."[24] In a courageous minority opinion, Marshall raged that the decision was a "cynical . . . grapeshot attack on race-conscious remedies."[25] But so it would continue in a long series of cases and new laws that limited the scope of equity programs and accelerated the undoing of desegregation.

Resegregation relied on the restoration of racial innocence, which absolved generations of their responsibility while allowing inequality to evolve and intensify. At the heart of the resegregationist turn was the same decoupling of cause and effect Powell had accomplished in the *Bakke* decision.

In 2007, in a case touching on issues of desegregation and diversity, *Parents Involved in Community Schools v. Seattle School District No. 1*, U.S. Supreme Court Chief Justice John Roberts concluded, "The way to stop discriminating on the basis of race is to stop discriminating on the basis of race."[26] Here was the natural limit of Powell's diversity rationale. If diversity is acceptable, not least because it entertains, edifies, and can be exploited, then why continue the charade around equity? Roberts's circular logic placed itself beyond rebuttal, admitted no light, refused all other ways of seeing and being. It was the sound of one side folding up and walking away from the race conversation.

In their minority opinion to *Bakke*, Justices Brennan, White, Marshall, and Blackmun had warned against the colorblindness that becomes "myopia which masks the reality that many 'created equal' have been treated within our lifetimes as inferior both by the law and by their fellow citizens." Marshall went on to cite the race gaps in life expectancy, and reminded his fellow justices that "the position of the Negro today in America is the tragic but inevitable consequence of centuries of unequal treatment." He argued, "In light of the sorry history of discrimination and its devastating impact on the lives of Negroes, bringing the Negro into the mainstream of American life should be a state interest of the highest order. To fail to do so is to ensure that America will forever remain a divided society."[27]

The distance between Marshall and Roberts is one way to map the *strangeness*—one of the root meanings of the Old French word "*diversité*"—of this current moment of polarization, the one side attaching inequality to history in order to warn of the consequences of reproducing inequity, the other side talking in circles. Diversity allows whites to remove themselves while requiring the Other to continue performing for them.

At the same moment that the courts, white legislators, and white voters were making the resegregationist turn, "diversity" suddenly became a buzzword. By 1996, Gingrich's Republicans declared that they were "the party of diversity." Diversity was good business. In 2000, Viacom purchased BET for $3 billion, to add to a portfolio that included Logo TV for the LGBT market, Nickelodeon for kids, and a bunch of channels for white males ages eighteen to thirty-four. Fourteen years later, Apple purchased Beats Electronics, the company founded by Dr. Dre and Jimmy Iovine, for $3 billion. Diversity became synonymous with profit making for all but the small businesses fighting for the right not to serve gay and transgender customers.

At the same time, while affirmative action programs were increasingly constrained by the courts and at the ballot box, public higher-ed technocrats tried to devise new programs to address continued underrepresentation of students of color. In Texas, Florida, and California, admissions processes were altered to include versions of what has been called the "Top Ten" method—accepting the talented top tenth (or fourth or some similar proportion) of the students of each high school.

As Justice Blackmun had predicted, such processes were not a perfect substitute for programs that directly addressed racial underrepresentation. Numbers of Black, Latino, and American Indian students dropped dramatically. Rapid demographic change alone would not guarantee that students of color would reach equitable numbers. On the contrary, in most cases, it only increased the urgency to find replacement plans for affirmative action. The innovation of the Top Ten plans was that they treated the best students from underfunded inner-city high schools equally with those from the well-funded exurban ones. Yet even after the states implemented these plans, most universities never returned to the level of diversity or equity they had attained before affirmative action programs were gutted.

Even worse, the plans were built on an irony that Thurgood Marshall himself might have found tragic. The Top Ten plans began with the assumption that high school students were already unequally distributed by race and class. Their success depended completely on school resegregation. The more segregated by race and income the state's high schools were, the better state universities would be able to create freshman diversity. In 1978, one rightly might have been dismayed by the desperation of such plans. But in three of the most racially diverse states in the country, there were no longer many other legal options to reverse resegregation in higher education.

Diverse Like You

What would Justice Marshall have thought of the halftime show of Super Bowl 50, which featured Beyoncé rocking a militant tribute to the Black Panther Party, accompanied by the quick-stepping Bruno Mars, a Filipino/Puerto Rican/Jewish son of Hawai'i, all but eclipsing the white rock headliner band, Coldplay. Would he have felt it was just another performance of diversity for whites? Would he have noted that only one of the thirty-two NFL team owners and only one of the top twenty power brokers in the music industry was of color?[28] People of color are allowed, even *required* to perform, and, especially these days on issues of race, to edify as well. *"Here you are now, entertain us."* But are we allowed to lead?

Business leaders from Silicon Valley to Hollywood to Wall Street trumpet the virtues of diversity, but still face protests over the lack of Black and brown faces in their offices and boardrooms. Other whites, including many who would describe themselves as far to the left of Trump, show signs of diversity fatigue.[29] As Anna Holmes has written of her white editors, who approach her to help them locate writers and editors of color, "I get the sense that for them, diversity is an end—a box to check off—rather than a starting point from which a more integrated, textured world is brought into being."[30]

The group that has benefited the most from the revolution of opportunity has been white women. In 1960, male college graduates outnumbered female grads by 60 percent. Those numbers have now reversed.[31] The gender pay gap persists, but during this ongoing "man-cession," many white women have been graduating directly into the most in-demand jobs in the economy. Affirmative action has helped white women close the income gap with white men.

Yet white women share their male counterparts' disdain for affirmative action, in similar numbers. The plaintiffs in all the major college affirmative action cases since *Bakke* have been white women. Younger whites are no more supportive of the program than older whites. Just one in three whites between the ages of seventeen and thirty-four support affirmative action, a negligible three percentage points higher than their elders.[32] If the court made diversity for white people, it would seem it is naive about how the law produces equity and reproduces inequity—or worse, perhaps, it no longer believes in equity at all.

Not long ago, I was asked to give a keynote speech for a Diversity Week at a large public university in a large state, that is to say, a campus about to become "majority minority" in a state about to become majority minority as well. I got into a discussion with the director of the multicultural center about how the week had been going. She said she was concerned that very few white students came to any of the week's events. They saw the word "diversity," she said, and decided to skip it. "Diversity" had become another word for "them," a new category of Otherness. Even the Academy of Motion Picture Arts and Sciences, in its recent effort to address the #OscarsSoWhite controversy, changed its rules to increase "the number of women and *diverse members*."[33]

And so diversity remains a premonition of racial apocalypse; a photo op and dash; a commodity conveying value; a marker of moral credibility, even fitness in the Darwinian sense; a term of corporate management; an offering of racial innocence and absolution; a refusal of protection to historically negated communities of color; a performance for entertainment or edification or exploitation; another boring lesson in tolerance and civility; a mark of Otherness.

But the fact that it appears as all of these things at once is yet another way to map the strangeness of this moment, or, to be more specific, the strangeness of whiteness. Demographic and cultural change has unsettled whites in their privilege. And so diversity presents itself as a lot of confused, contradictory things at once, each indexed to the confused, contradictory states of whites themselves.

Yet these are not the only meanings that diversity necessarily need hold. Is it possible to reimagine diversity separated from histories of exclusion? What would diversity that liberated everyone look like?

WHAT A TIME TO BE ALIVE

ON STUDENT PROTEST

When Jonathan Butler began his hunger strike at the University of Missouri in November of 2015 to force President Tim Wolfe to resign, an action Butler said was precipitated by the president's inattention to what student protesters called "racial violence and exclusivity," he had been at the school longer than the administrator had.

President Wolfe had been at Mizzou for three years. Twenty-five-year-old Jonathan Butler had been a student at the university for seven. He had secured his bachelor's degree there and was nearing completion of a master's degree in education. He had been on campus long enough to believe that things were not going to get better unless something dramatic happened.

Butler told CNN, "I felt unsafe since the moment I stepped on this campus." But rather than run, he chose to protest. "We love Mizzou enough to critique and to fight against the injustices we face at this school."[1]

After Butler's weeklong hunger strike, which climaxed when the Mizzou football team threatened not to play, Wolfe stepped down. But though the protests at Mizzou ended, the fire quickly burned outward from the prairie, fueled by the winds of social media, following the spread of the Movement for Black Lives from Ferguson the year before. In all, during the 2015–16 school year, nearly one hundred universities and colleges would receive lists of demands from students demonstrating for racial equity.

Predictably, both conservative and liberal pundits decried the new wave of antiracist campus activism. On the right, the *National Review*'s David French called them "revolutionaries" who sought "nothing less than the overthrow of our constitutional republic, beginning with our universities."[2] The liberal critique was even more bizarre, a barely coherent mix of free-speech absolutism (*hate speech is valuable because you had to respond to it*), pop-psych generational stereotype (*oh, you narcissistic, entitled millennials*), and "moderate" triumphalism (*look how crazy you extremists on the left and the right are!*).

At the *Atlantic*, Conor Friedersdorf called student organizers "intolerant bullies." Todd Gitlin wondered in the *New York Times* why they felt so vulnerable and fearful. Thomas Friedman wrote, "There is surely a connection between the explosion of political correctness on college campuses—including Yale students demanding the resignation of an administrator whose wife defended free speech norms that might make some students uncomfortable—and the ovations Donald Trump is getting for being crudely politically incorrect."[3]

To be fair, in a season of righteous student unrest, there were lots of examples of hyperbole. Pundits had a field day with Oberlin, where students protested botched dining hall sushi and bánh mì. But while those incidents were funny, they hardly threatened free speech. When administrators made suggestions not to wear certain culturally appropriating gear on Halloween, it hardly signaled the end of Western civilization. They might have made the day more tolerable, maybe even preemptively stopped some buzz-killing confrontations. Culture matters, context matters, and cultural context matters.

So were student protesters a mob of anti–free speech thugs or a confused mass of coddled dependents? Of course they were neither.

When students protested, it was not anti–free speech, it was the practice of free speech. Critics drew a direct line between protest and censorship, but speaking up about injustice is exactly what democracy is supposed to look like. What Jelani Cobb called "the free speech diversion" was meant to shut down the intended discussion.[4]

Over the last quarter century of student protest against racism, the act of calling out so-called political correctness has become a standard strategy of silencing. The legal scholar Mari Matsuda reminds us that racial attacks and hate speech, as well as the "anti-PC" defense of them, are proof that free speech is not a neutral good equally available to all. "The places where the law does not go to redress harm have tended to be the places where women, children, people of color, and poor people live," she has written. "Tolerance of hate speech is not tolerance borne by the community at large. Rather, it is a psychic tax imposed on those least able to pay."[5]

But even liberals who pride themselves on their antiracism have their own ways of trying to get the protesters to turn down, as it were. They draw false equivalencies—equating student protests against institutional racism with the ending of free speech, as if calling out racism were the same as issuing a racist call to extremism. At least conservative critics don't pretend to be ignorant of how power works. Student activists rightly believe that they can build power only insofar as they band together—and then they can still be ignored, as they mostly always have been. Institutional neglect of racism and injustice is the exercise of power, the kind of power that refuses to notice and refuses to speak.

Protest of moral and historic force begins with people facing extreme vulnerability. For those who have been silenced, rising to the act of speaking is a perilously high climb indeed. For them, protest is not an expression of fear and doubt, but an overcoming of fear and doubt. And when it comes from those at the bottom, it can often be a profound proposition about how to make the world better for all. That's the difference between the mob whipped into a frenzy by a demagogue and the protesters demanding that institutions address harmful conditions that negate their very existence. One excludes, the other raises up.

I have written elsewhere that while we are engaged in the culture wars, the most difficult thing to do is keep the "race conversation" going, because its polarizing modalities are better at teaching us what not to say to each other than what to say, better at closing off conversation than starting it. In this way those who believe that protesters are dangerous and those who believe they are merely misguided join together to end the necessary discussion the rest of us might want to have, in fact need to have. If the choice is framed as one of silence versus noise, in the long run most people prefer silence.

Here we might take a lesson from two people who helped to bring about the peaceful end of apartheid in South Africa. The first was a white Afrikaner named Roelf Meyer, who served as the National Party's vice minister of police during the national state of emergency from 1985 to 1988. His job was to stop the demonstrations in the Black townships by any means necessary. But as he came to understand the suffering of Blacks and Coloureds under the apartheid regime, he underwent a profound change of heart, and emerged by the end of the decade as one of the key voices for change within the party. He became the chief negotiator for the de Klerk government to bring apartheid to an end, eventually becoming so respected and trusted that Nelson Mandela would later offer him a position in the new government.

As he engaged in this process, he was met with derision from fellow Afrikaners. They called him a traitor and worse. They asked how he could be so concerned with the freedom of Black people. They told him he had ruined his life and those of his fellow whites. And he responded that they had it exactly wrong. "I have liberated myself," he told them, "and we have liberated ourselves." He deliberately echoed Martin Luther King Jr., who famously wrote, "Injustice anywhere is a threat to justice everywhere. We are caught in an inescapable network of mutuality, tied in a single garment of destiny."[6]

One of the men on the other side of the table was a Coloured Muslim named Ebrahim Rasool. He would go on to become South Africa's ambassador to the United States. During the time Meyer was police chief, Rasool had been in solitary confinement because of his activism with the African National Congress. Rasool had every right to be bitter and angry.

But as followers of Mandela, Rasool and others in the ANC came to believe that a process of truth and reconciliation needed to be a key part of the country's transition to democracy. The truth would be difficult to speak, but it would be necessary to begin to right the wrongs done to Blacks and Coloureds. Reconciliation would not be a gift, but "an exchange for truth."[7]

In other words, peace and justice are inseparable from each other. If the Black and Coloured majority pressed only for justice, it might be doomed to the violent cycle of retribution. If it pressed only for peace, it might sacrifice justice and be doomed to the violence of inequality. It needed to pursue both at the same time, through a moral process with a moral end. This understanding echoed another of King's ideas: "True peace is not merely the absence of tension; it is the presence of justice."[8]

I am not trying to compare relative racisms here. I'm proposing a way to recognize and approach the accumulation and reaccumulation of inequity, which does happen along a spectrum—from unintended offense to racial violence.

Those whose first response to protest is to lecture demonstrators about how students ought to protest signal an utter disdain for the why of the protest. Lost in all the bluster about how students should just grow the f up and also accept everything their liberal professors tell them—contradictory, right?—is a simple truth: campuses, like the country itself, are seeing rising levels of hate and intolerance, the tragic result of over a quarter century of intensifying racial inequality and resegregation and a silence over these selfsame issues.

In 2013 alone, Oberlin, Dartmouth, Carleton College, and the University of California at Irvine were all shaken by reports of racial incidents. Oberlin held a campus-wide convocation on the question of racism and campus climate. When two liberal students were detained and confessed to having caused some of the incidents, conservative websites gleefully reported the arrests as proof of "imaginary racism" and evidence that most campus hate crimes were hoaxes. But Oberlin police had also documented a long list of incidents, threats, and posts that had occurred, the administration said, "on a virtually daily basis over a period of weeks."

Many wondered how all of this could be happening at small, progressive liberal arts schools. But the following year the protests spread to larger universities. Black students at Harvard, the University of Michigan, and UCLA called attention to campus racism and the personal toll of ongoing underrepresentation. The question became: Are we witnessing a national trend? By 2015, the student uprisings had proven that the answer definitively was yes.

Across the country, no matter what kind of college or university, student demands were surprisingly consistent—more faculty and staff of color, stronger curriculum around difference and inclusion, redoubled efforts to increase recruitment and retention of students, faculty, and staff of color, increased funding for multicultural centers, greater attention to relations with local communities, more diversity training for faculty and staff, the hiring of diversity officers and culturally competent counseling and mental health professionals.[9]

There are two points to be made here. The first is that the strengthening of speech codes was by far one of the least common demands.[10] "Media has really taken a liking to the narrative that protestors . . . seek to be coddled," one student, Aryn Frazier, the president of University of Virginia's Black Student Alliance, told Emma Pierson and Leah Pierson, two student researchers who analyzed the demands. "If anything, the reason black students are protesting is because they have been the opposite of coddled—they have been ignored and silenced and hurt by people and systems at their universities."[11]

More important, the top demands were consistent with demands that have been made by students of color for *three decades* now. To the extent that student protest has entered the national narrative, it has been confined mainly to the sixties, a kind of Greatest Generation story about upheaval in cultural norms, mostly starring white boomer men. But historians of the next century may look back to the period that followed as the one in which young people truly reshaped the culture—especially where, because of demographic and social shifts, the category of youth intersected with race, class, and identity. The story of higher education during this period, that place where all of those explosive strands came together, should play an outsize role.

Historically white universities and colleges came to include and accommodate students of color only after two major waves of intense activism. The first began in the mid-1960s in reaction to the rise of the civil rights movement and accelerated after the 1968 Third World Liberation Front strike at San Francisco State College catalyzed the founding of Black studies and ethnic studies programs and the rapid expansion of affirmative action.

The second wave began in the mid-1980s, when students of color became majorities or large pluralities at many campuses. Young activists reacted to the rising tide of hate incidents by demonstrating for the hiring of more faculty and staff of color, demanding that universities create and expand multicultural centers and diversity programs, and redefining the bounds of civility to foster environments of inclusion.

The bureaucratic term for all of this racialized unrest— both the tensions and the protests they generated—was "campus climate," popularized in an influential 1992 article by Sylvia Hurtado, a University of Michigan professor. Hurtado, a Chicana who had attended Harvard and Princeton, led with a sobering finding that racial conflict had become "commonplace on American college campuses throughout the 1980s." In 1988 and 1989 alone, she wrote, there were "more than one hundred college campuses reporting incidents of racial/ethnic harassment and violence." She added, "Instances of overt racial conflict can no longer be viewed as aberrations or isolated incidents, but rather [as] indicators of a more general problem of unresolved racial issues in college environments and in society at large."[12]

Student protests became so widespread that they forced administrations to react. Research universities, especially the flagship public schools, led the way in expanding multicultural and diversity programs. But a backlash formed among both liberals and conservatives.

In a 1992 *Time* magazine cover story on "The Fraying of America," later expanded into a best-selling book-length polemic, the art critic Robert Hughes decried "the culture of complaint," in which multiculturalists and moral majoritarians marched the nation toward irreparable fragmentation.[13] The militantly unironic arch-conservative Dinesh D'Souza—who first gained notice when as a Dartmouth student he took a sledgehammer to an anti-apartheid shantytown—titled his own anti-antiracist book *Illiberal Education*. Writing of the 1989 Howard University protests against the seating of Republican strategist Lee Atwater on the school's board of trustees, D'Souza called them "a kind of collective tantrum aimed at getting attention" and argued, "What [students] need from the university is not coddling and illusion, but intellectual and moral leadership to prepare them for the challenges they must face as adults."[14] (In this regard, Friedersdorf, Gitlin, Friedman, and French were simply regurgitating tired old culture-war arguments.)

Demography and time proved Hughes and D'Souza wrong. The union did not go the way of the Balkans. On the other hand, the culture warriors did succeed in one regard: their objections cowed universities into moving away from actively addressing campus climate and racial equity.

When attacks on affirmative action intensified in the mid-nineties, some university leaders took high-profile stands to defend it. By then, diversity had proven value. It looked great to prospective students, and demographics counted in the annual college rankings. But there has been less reward in taking care of the students of color who are actually admitted. Inclusion requires attention, which requires staffing and policies and commitment, and it also requires mobilizing tenured faculty, which is like herding moody, drowsy lions.

Beginning in the 2000s, campuses increasingly turned to businessmen to preside over downsizing. When universities should have been turning to enlightened leadership ready to tackle the challenges of a colorizing nation, they instead sought out ruthless corporate types who specialized in market positioning and cost-cutting.

Nearly two decades later, universities continued to function under an austerity mind-set that focused on financial goals over educational missions. The University of Missouri had brought in Tim Wolfe from a software company that had just been flipped. He had no academic experience. Board members expected him to grow and market the university's "value." At Mount St. Mary's University, in Maryland, President Simon Newman, a former private-equity investor, was forced out after trying to implement a plan to improve the school's retention numbers by pushing struggling students to drop out. He told a professor, "You think of the students as cuddly bunnies. But you can't. You just have to drown the bunnies . . . put a Glock to their heads."[15]

During this period, ethnic studies programs and multicultural student services across the country were frozen or slashed. Staff and faculty of color who survived told stories behind closed doors about being the last to be hired, the first to be photographed for the brochures, and the first to be cut. And yet demographics didn't stop. So in the face of another and yet another "most diverse generation ever," universities continued to admit fewer Black and brown students and provided them with less support than ever.

When Sylvia Hurtado first wrote about campus climate, in 1992, she noted that one in four students perceived considerable racial conflict at their universities. Larger pluralities of all students felt that universities were doing little to resolve the problem.

In 2012, a system-wide survey of over 100,000 students, staff, and faculty by the University of California found that one in four respondents "had personally experienced exclusionary, intimidating, offensive, and/or hostile conduct" on campus.[16] Underrepresented minorities, transgender and gender-queer, and undocumented students were much more likely than other students to feel uncomfortable in classes, to have experienced exclusionary conduct, and to state that they did not see enough faculty and staff with whom they identified. One in four students of color and queer students had at some point seriously considered dropping out, compared to less than one in five white students.

What kind of personal toll did this take on those students? The burden of representation—the idea that one has to always attend to the gap between how one appears to others and how one perceives oneself—had always been real. The social psychologist Claude Steele called this "stereotype threat," and argued that it accounted for the intense pressure Black and brown students faced in the classroom. After affirmative action was struck down across the country, stereotype threat also explained why the most competitive Black and Latino students declined admission offers at places where affirmative action had been gutted, like the University of California and University of Michigan, and instead gathered at historically Black colleges and universities and those private, elite universities that promised community and support. Students increasingly sought what they called, using the language of trauma and recovery, "safe spaces."

And how might they navigate the new minefield between "diversity is good" cheerleading and the reality of still-hostile, inequitable environments? During the 1980s and 1990s, an ambience of hostility—from slurs carved into bathroom walls to racist Greek-system theme parties—had fueled student protests. "Campus climate" gave universities language to address their changing student bodies. But by the late 2000s, institutionalized diversity and post-racial colorblindness had created a broadly untenable situation for students of color. If hate incidents occurred, university officials and individuals would routinely condemn them. To be fair, "This is not who we are" was an improvement upon "You're not like us." But most universities were no better than the rest of the nation at avoiding the same old cycle around race of crisis, reaction, backlash, and complacency. And still, demographics don't stop.

In order to describe the campus racism of the "postracial" moment, students turned to Columbia University scholar Derald Wing Sue, who was reviving Harvard psychiatrist Chester Pierce's Black Power–era notion of microaggressions. Microaggressions were not the same as hate speech or physical violence. They were the moments of daily indignity that, as Sue and his colleagues wrote, "communicate hostile, derogatory, or negative racial slights and insults to the target person or group."[17] In 1970 Pierce had written, "Most offensive actions are not gross and crippling. They are subtle and stunning. The enormity of the complications they cause can be appreciated only when one considers that these subtle blows are delivered incessantly."[18]

In 2010, two Columbia University students named Vivian Lu and David Zhou, angry about racist and sexist flyers distributed by candidates for student government, began a Tumblr blog called *The Microaggressions Project* to document the regular indignities they and their classmates faced. "Being able to identify what these uncomfortable and sometimes painful situations are," Lu, Zhou, and other members of the project later wrote, "is the first step in changing the society that causes individuals to express ideas that bias and discriminate."[19]

The idea quickly went viral. Hundreds of other students on dozens of other campuses set up their own blogs and began organizing activist work around them. In time, discussions over microaggressions had spread from the campuses into the mainstream, and the American Dialect Society declared the word itself one of the "most useful" words of 2015.[20] The language of microaggressions gave students of the "post-racial" moment a way to talk about the gap between society's regular celebrations of diversity and its continuing inequality.

With the killings of Trayvon Martin and Michael Brown, a generation that had grown up during an era of rising resegregation and inequality could see how the microaggressions they experienced in often elite collegiate spaces connected to a broader context of racial inequity. What's more, Tumblr, Twitter, and Facebook helped them not only to make their local struggles visible, but to recognize that they fit into a larger national narrative of rising anger over inequity. Social media and the Internet accelerated generational learning and mobilization. They had the tools, language, infrastructure, and the belly-fire to respond to what felt like a deteriorating situation. And then Mizzou happened.

In 2008, Jonathan Butler came to the University of Missouri from North Omaha, Nebraska. He had been raised in a family of ministers and lawyers, who were deeply active in the life of the city's Black community. As a teenager he had been engaged in prison ministry. He believed in what he called the idea of "sacrificing yourself for the betterment of others." When he got to Mizzou, he said he felt "culture shock."

He was one of two Black men in his dorm. He and his friend Joseph found themselves talking to each other about being bullied in their engineering classes and called racial slurs as they walked across campus. The week before the presidential elections, Obama came to campus to rally students and all seemed well. Yet Butler also felt tensions developing. Some white students seemed to feel threatened by the prospect of a Black president.

On the night of the election, Joseph went home to Chicago to be with his family for the historic moment. Butler was the only Black male in his dorm. He hid in his room watching the news. When they called it for Obama, he ran into the hallway and began celebrating. No one else was there to join him. But three white men at the end of the hall came over and angrily confronted him. "They had already been drinking, you could smell it from their breaths," Butler recalled. "They came and they attacked me." He took several punches before another friend pulled him out of the hallway and back into his room. Later, the *n*-word was scrawled on his dorm-room door.

Over Butler's next seven years at Mizzou, the Gaines/Oldham Black Culture Center was vandalized with cotton balls during Black History Month; a swastika was drawn in ashes on a residence hall wall; and the swimmer Sasha Menu Courey committed suicide after the school failed to address her claims that she had been sexually assaulted. Butler saw a university that did not take Black student concerns seriously. He told Greg E. Hill of the *Minority Trailblazers* podcast, "No one wants to believe us. No one wants to listen to us when we're at diversity forums. No one wants to listen to us when we're having one-on-one conversations with faculty, staff, and administrators. No one wants to listen to us when we're sending emails."[21]

Butler added, "Everyone wants Black students to be respectable and 'civilized' and go through the 'proper channels.' But here [with Sasha Menu Courey] you have a prime example of someone who went through the 'proper channels,' went through an extremely traumatic incident, and then you still don't have them being valued as their own human life."

When Ferguson happened, Butler and other students frequently traveled the two hours from campus to join the protests. Many also took part in the nonviolent direct action trainings. Three Black queer students formed MU for Michael Brown, the precursor to #ConcernedStudent1950, an organization that they named for the year the first Black student was accepted into the university. The group became the primary engine for the feverish campus organizing that began in the fall of 2015.

The Mizzou demonstrations brought together a number of strands of protest, including concerns about sexual assault, grad student health-care cuts, Islamophobia on campus, and restrictions against student use of Planned Parenthood. But they accelerated with campus climate issues. At the outset of the 2015–16 school year, student body president Peyton Head was taunted with racial slurs in the street. The Legion of Black Collegians' homecoming rally was interrupted by another student yelling slurs. And when university president Tim Wolfe ignored student protesters at a homecoming parade, #ConcernedStudent1950 issued a list of demands starting with Wolfe's removal and continuing with "inclusion curriculum," increases in Black faculty and staff, and resources for the mental health and social justice centers.

After a second swastika—this time made of feces— was drawn on a residence hall wall, and Wolfe continued to voice his ignorance of campus climate concerns, Butler signed a Do Not Resuscitate order and began his hunger strike. During the week that followed, Black students escalated their protests by opening an encampment on Carnahan Quad, encountering increased racial harassment in person and death threats online.

A group of students confronted Wolfe as he left a meeting. One asked him to define "systematic oppression." His answer was not just insensitive, it seemed anti-intellectual: "Systematic oppression is because you don't believe you have the equal opportunity for success." Students peppered him with more questions: "Did you just blame us for systematic oppression, Tim Wolfe? Did you just blame Black students?" Wolfe turned and quickly walked away. When the Mizzou football team joined the protests via a Twitter photo—threatening a boycott that had the potential to cost the school $1 million per game—Wolfe and Chancellor R. Bowen Loftin resigned.[22]

Not long afterward, more than fifty-five years to the day that the first Black student was admitted to the University of Missouri, the campus established the Office for Civil Rights and Title IX to centralize the investigation of discrimination complaints. That delayed and still inadequate action, the imperial obfuscation and denial, the need to dramatically increase the stakes—these were some of the strategies of denial that students had been trying to call attention to all along.

For Jonathan Butler, that point had been worth the final sacrifice. "The contemporary Black Lives movement moment that we are in right now wasn't founded by any individuals. It was founded by the lives of Trayvon Martin, by the lives of Mike Brown, by Rekia Boyd, and so many others. It really showed me you just can't play around with it. This is serious, this is systemic, and we have to fight it at all costs."

Youth movements are always fueled by a combustible mix of pain, defiance, imagination, inexperience, commitment, and risk. The most successful of them turn what look to elders like insurmountable liabilities into virtues. The most moral of them open up new ways to see how we can live better together.

Resegregation happens through design and through apathy. It also grows through our blindness—whether willed, imperceivable, or fixed through the best of our intentions—to the deep connections between us all. Silence over resegregation has led us to this historical moment. The young may not speak in the language we are accustomed to hearing. We may think them sometimes too imprecise or cavalier in their rage. But if we miss their point—for which they have been willing to sacrifice everything—we will undoubtedly be hearing it again from the next generation.

THE ODDS

ON CULTURAL EQUITY

When the Academy Awards came around in the second year of #OscarsSoWhite, I decided I would support Spike and Jada's boycott—my little twenty-first-century version of honoring the picket line, engaging by disengaging. But in this era of converging media, there is no escaping Big Cultural Events. When my friend Kai texted me, I could no longer ignore the damn thing. "Yikes," she wrote. "Jose sparked a POC fight on Twitter about anti-Blackness."

Jose was our friend Jose Antonio Vargas, the indefatigable undocumented Pinoy activist who at that moment was one of the main targets of a brilliant and viciously funny Black Twitter hashtag #NotYourMule.

As Chris Rock worked through his opening monologue, Jose had tweeted, "When will @chrisrock bring up Latino, Asian, Middle Eastern, Native American actors and opportunity?" Others, it turned out, were wondering the same thing. Ming-Na Wen tweeted, "Chris Rock hasn't once brought up other minorities who have worse odds at the #Oscars." Black writer and activist Mikki Kendall replied, "Someone tell me not to do a #NotYourMule tag about the expectation that Black people take all the risk to advance representation in media."[1]

Kendall had summoned Zora Neale Hurston—the

patron saint of Black Twitter, the respectability-politics-exploding writer-fighter who knew her way around an incisive diss. In *Their Eyes Were Watching God*, Hurston's character Nanny declares, "De nigger woman is de mule uh de world so fur as Ah can see." Kendall's hashtag set the feeds flying—tweets about Black solidarity for POC, POC anti-Black racism, Peter Liang, it was all on the table.

In its 2016 nominations, the Academy ignored what might be called the Black Lives renaissance—the broad, urgent work of Black actors, directors, and others who were telling some of the most important stories of our time. It was the second year in a row that April Reign's #OscarsSoWhite hashtag mobilized audience fury at the blatant omissions.

In response, Academy head Cheryl Boone Isaacs, the first woman of color ever to hold the position, pushed her board to pass a plan "doubling the membership of women and diverse members of the Academy by 2020."[2] The actors' branch alone was 88 percent white. Even the Academy's language of change was awkward and out of touch, directed largely at convincing its "non-diverse" members. Here was another American institution, led by a Black woman, whose leadership and membership remained unrepresentative of and unresponsive to a constituency that had changed. The story sounded Clinton Sparks familiar.

In fact, it reminded Jose of a 2014 *Hollywood Reporter* cover essay written by Chris Rock, packaged under the headline IT'S A WHITE INDUSTRY. IT JUST IS. In it, Rock wrote personally and passionately about his efforts to create opportunities for other Black actors and artists in a closed studio system. Jose had been particularly struck by two paragraphs.

"But forget whether Hollywood is black enough," Rock wrote. "A better question is: Is Hollywood Mexican enough?" He continued:

> You're in L.A., you've got to *try* not to hire Mexicans. It's the most liberal town in the world, and there's a part of it that's kind of racist—not racist like "F—you, nigger" racist, but just an acceptance that there's a slave state in L.A. There's this acceptance that Mexicans are going to take care of white people in L.A. that doesn't exist anywhere else. . . .
>
> You're telling me no Mexicans are qualified to do anything at a studio? Really? Nothing but mop up? What are the odds that that's true? The odds are, because people are people, that there's probably a Mexican David Geffen mopping up for somebody's company right now.[3]

Jose had been so moved that he and his team produced a powerful video, "I, Too," for his EmergingUS platform that they debuted the day of the Oscars. It seemed to have been inspired by Coca-Cola's 2014 Super Bowl ad, "America the Beautiful." But in his piece there was no cynical ploy to sell sugar water. Instead the video offered beautiful images of Latinos in Los Angeles—a parking lot flagger, a taquería food worker, a seamstress, a deliveryman, an elderly worker on a bus, a young mother and her child—all set to the sound of a man reciting in Spanish Langston Hughes's famous poem "Yo también canto América."

Jose later recalled, "When Rock started his monologue, I thought maybe he'd repeat a line or two from his essay." So he tweeted his question. But as the night and the feeds rolled on, he realized that Kendall and others were likely reading something else into it—a misplaced anger about Rock's omission, or, worse, an aggrandizing "what about me" ethnic solipsism, an expression of non-Black POC entitlement. As Kendall put it, "Solidarity doesn't look like Black people taking the risks & everyone else reaping the rewards."[4]

If Twitter's brevity does nuance no favors, its velocity can reveal complexity very quickly. When #OscarsSo-White gave way to #NotYourMule, the discussion branched from the whiteness of Hollywood to the relative invisibility of different communities of color. But both hashtags also reminded non-Black people of color of the central role Black protest and creative expression has played in moving us all toward cultural equity. After all, "I, Too" had reappropriated Langston Hughes. For years, Black directors, producers, and writers had been the champions of opportunities for other non-whites. Jose knew all of this very well. By the next day, the conversation had moved beyond whiteness and invisibility to the stakes in the struggle for equity. It is the continuing strangeness and difficulty of race that all of these conversations have to happen at the same time.

But we must begin somewhere. So let us start with the whiteness of Hollywood. American popular culture, by its nature, trades on optimism. It wants spectacle with its trauma. It wants its laughs, its happy endings. This is the legacy of a national culture birthed in the twin narratives of cowboys-and-Indians and blackface minstrelsy.

It may also be true that we have entered into a new golden age of representation. Many of our biggest icons are people of color. Our pop landscape appears desegregated. Take television. For about a decade, from the mid-

1980s through the mid-1990s, networks featured shows that centered on Black lives, from the groundbreaking *Cosby Show* to *Living Single*. But by the turn of the millennium, shows like *Girlfriends* and *George Lopez* were the exception. Cable picked up the slack, making stars of Dave Chappelle and Tyler Perry, and telling important stories on shows such as *The Wire* and *The Shield*. On the networks, characters of color had come to appear mostly in big ensemble shows, giving emergency rooms and criminal courts their verisimilitude of diversity. These were images of a "post-racial" America, mostly featuring middle-class people of color who were just like middle-class white people, except for the color of their skin.

In the first year of Obama's presidency, ABC's *Modern Family* reconstructed the suburban sitcom by augmenting the stock white nuclear family with an extended clan that featured a gay couple with an adopted Asian American child, and a patriarch with a gorgeous young Latina wife and child. In Hollywood elevator-pitch terms, it was *Married with Children* meets *I Love Lucy* and *The Birdcage*. But its surprise success made it possible for TV execs to gingerly step back toward shows with leads of color. For twenty years, Asians had not had a lead on television, but in 2016 *Fresh Off the Boat*, *Quantico*, and *Dr. Ken* were among ABC's top shows. ABC was also home to *Black-ish* and Shonda Rhimes's *Scandal* and *How to Get Away With Murder*. On Fox, *Empire* continued to crush the ratings. They were *the* big stories in a company town that loves to celebrate its successes.

So maybe it seems a bit rude, a bit vibe-killing to note that, despite all of this, Hollywood remains overwhelmingly white. But it does. In February 2016, when Channing Dungey, an African American woman, was named president of ABC Entertainment, she became the first person of color to head a major network. In 2014, less than 6 percent of executive producers and 14 percent of writers were of color.[5] These numbers had barely changed in a decade. Hollywood may indeed be run by the most liberal whites in the country—some of them have written and acted and produced with the deepest of empathy. But they can never be a substitute for people who can tell their own stories best. That was the lesson of *Black-ish*, *Fresh Off the Boat*, and *Empire*'s breakthroughs, a lesson that needed to be relearned every twenty years or so. Millions wanted to see shows written, directed, and acted by people of color telling stories about themselves. Duh.

And yet the odds of a person of color breaking into the upper echelon of the culture, where the stories and songs and visions that we tell ourselves about ourselves—with all their values, meanings, and instructions for living—are gathered, made, and produced, and then marketed, sold, and pushed back to us, remain long indeed.

Culture, like food, is necessary to sustain us. It molds us and shapes our relations to each other. An inequitable culture is one in which people do not have the same power to create, access, or circulate their practices, works, ideas, and stories. It is one in which people cannot represent themselves equally. To say that American culture is inequitable is to say that it moves us away from seeing each other in our full humanity. It is to say that the culture does not point us toward a more just society.

Artists and activists have long demanded better representation for people of color, women, poor people, and rural people. They have asked: Who is represented in and through cultural production? How does their representation, underrepresentation, or misrepresentation undo or reproduce various forms of inequality? But cultural equity is not just about representation. It is also about access and power. How can important cultural knowledge survive? Who has access to the means of production of culture? Who has the power to shape culture?

By the end of the twentieth century most developed countries had established modern structures to support the production of culture. Funding for the arts came through four primary sectors: the state, the culture industry, philanthropy, and community.

Culture was an important tool to develop and project a national identity. Democratic countries such as Canada, New Zealand, South Korea, and Denmark funded the development of large cultural sectors through government ministries. But such state-sponsored cultural production did not necessarily imply the building of propaganda machines. That false narrative was a peculiar product of the Cold War and the culture wars.

In fact, before the Cold War, the United States led the world in building a robust, democratic cultural policy. The New Deal supported the art and the artists who created the enduring images, stories, and songs of the "American century." Zora Neale Hurston, Dorothea Lange, Orson Welles, Charles White, Ralph Ellison, and Richard Wright were all beneficiaries. The artists exposed inequality in America. They forged a new national narrative that wielded values of inclusion and resilience against hardship and despair.

The culture industry reacted belatedly to this shift. Popular movies reflecting progressive values like *It's a Wonderful Life* or *On the Waterfront* came long after the peak of the cultural front. At any rate, the Hollywood blacklist campaigns brought an end to this period of rich expression, illustrating how sensitive industry leaders were to the pressures of being labeled "red." By itself, a culture industry concerned with a bottom line or political pressures would not lead toward equity.

As an answer to Soviet soft power, President Johnson established the National Endowment for the Arts and the National Endowment for the Humanities in 1965. The NEA played a key role in funding the growth of fledgling institutions that made up the arts uprisings of the 1970s and 1980s. At its peak, the NEA controlled the equivalent of half a billion 2015 dollars annually, and ecosystems of arts organizations from Appalachia to Los Angeles produced a generation of artists of color and women, queer, and avant-garde artists who would popularize multiculturalist ideas.[6]

But after the fall of the Soviet Union, right-wing moralists attacked these same artists and ecosystems by vowing to defund the NEA and NEH. By the mid-nineties, they had succeeded in forcing many arts organizations to close shop. Conservatives argued at the time that if an artist could not find someone to pay for their art, or fund it themselves, then maybe it did not deserve to be made. Consolidation of the culture industry followed. George Yudice has famously called this moment "the privatization of culture."[7]

By the end of the 2000s, New Zealand, a country that is seventy times smaller than the United States, was appropriating $50 million more to its Ministry for Culture and Heritage than the United States was to the NEA. Between 2000 and 2010, state funding for the arts dropped by over a billion dollars.

Inequality in the American arts world now is more severe than even income inequality. Nationally, the top

20 percent of income earners receive 50 percent of the income. In the U.S. arts world, the top 2 percent of organizations garner 55 percent of philanthropic grants. Seventy-five percent of organizations serving underrepresented populations have budgets of under $250,000.[8]

Of every foundation dollar given in the United States, only eleven cents goes to the arts. Five and a half cents goes to arts organizations with budgets of more than five million dollars. One cent goes to arts organizations serving underrepresented communities. Less than half a cent goes to arts organizations that produce work related to social justice.[9]

For the last decade, many of the largest nonprofit arts institutions have been confronting the vexing question of "audience," namely the steep declines in aging white patrons. Yet many of these same arts institutions seem to have little interest in questions of equity and instead seem to be positioning themselves to follow their narrowing audiences down into oblivion. It is too early to know if crowdfunding, the for-profit version of the age-old sweat-equity model so popular in the 1960s and 1970s, can be of service in the push for cultural equity. On the one hand, here is where cultural moves always start: with the enthusiasm of creation, in the spirit of beating the odds. But the odds remain what they are.

History reminds us that desegregation is not a destination; it is a constant struggle. It took until 2015 for the Emmys to honor a Black leading lady. "The only thing that separates women of color from anyone else is opportunity," said Viola Davis, the star of *How to Get Away with Murder*, upon winning her award. "You cannot win an

Emmy for roles that are simply not there." Spike Lee, who received a 2015 honorary Oscar for lifetime achievement before the nominations angered him into boycotting the February ceremonies, said in his acceptance speech, "It's easier to be the president of the United States as a black person than to be the head of a studio."[10]

For decades, the problem was not even seen as a problem. Only in light of the justice movements and rising cultural activism have many of the art world's and culture industry's leaders tried to address the problem.

One sign is the recent flood of reports documenting the extent of cultural inequity. Here's a short list of their recent (re)discoveries:

- 87 percent of American museum leaders, curators, conservators, and educators are white. More than half of security and facilities workers are nonwhite.[11]
- Of the largest museums, theaters, and dance companies in the United States, none have annual budgets of less than $23 million. Of the twenty largest African American and Latino museums, theaters, and dance companies in the United States, only five have annual budgets of more than $5 million.[12]
- In a survey of over 1,000 New York City arts organizations, 69 percent of those polled agreed or strongly agreed with the statement "I feel my organization is diverse." Yet 78 percent of board members and 79 percent of leadership staff in these same organizations were white. The city is 33 percent white.[13]

And yet access and representation are only a part of the problem of cultural equity. Even if these issues are addressed, the question of power will remain. In a world that is no longer white, to borrow from James Baldwin, will the culture point us toward greater understanding and justice, or will it reproduce social inequities?

These questions had Jose Antonio Vargas disheartened the day after the Oscars. He worried that some might have mistaken his intentions. Two days later he posted an essay he had written entitled "Here's What I've Learned About #NotYourMule."[14]

First, he wrote that while "it would have been helpful," he now felt Chris Rock was in no way obligated to speak for non-Blacks. Indeed, as the discussion had proceeded during the Oscars ceremony, Latinos and Asian Americans started their own hashtags to focus on underrepresentation. He concluded by saying that he did not believe that race was solely a "Black vs White" issue, but that he vowed to address anti-Black racism in his future work. He wrote, ". . . white people don't always need to be at the center of the conversation."

But there was more racial controversy lingering from the Oscars, in the form of tone-deaf jokes Sacha Baron Cohen and Chris Rock told at the expense of Asians. Rock had tried to inject some humor into a required segment about the accountants' tabulation of the votes. "They sent us their most dedicated, accurate, and hardworking representatives. Please welcome Ming Zhu, Bao Ling, and David Moskowitz," he said, as three Asian American kids carrying briefcases walked onstage to laughter and not a few groans.

"If anybody's upset about that joke," Rock added, "just tweet about it on your phone that was also made by these kids."

Cohen's joke was delivered—unscripted and unapproved by show producers—in character as British wigga Ali G. "Here comes yet another token Black presenter," he began. He went on to say, "How come there is no Oscar for them really hardworking tiny yellow people with no dongs? You know, Minions."

As with Sarah Silverman's skits circa 2003–04, Cohen's "post-racial" humor turned on the shock value of saying racist things in a faux-clueless manner to an audience that knew they were racist jokes told by white liberals for white liberals. Audiences could indulge in the communal thrill of laughing at the stereotypes while staying safely above it all. Here again was why white Hollywood liberalism could never be a substitute for cultural equity.

Chris Rock understood this problem well. The power in his art, like Dave Chappelle's and Patrice O'Neal's, came from dancing on the line between white flattery and Black truth. There was one way in which Rock's Asian joke might have been made subversive, become the kind of grace note that Jose had been seeking. It might have made the joke, worthy of Rock's cutting intelligence, something funny and uncomfortable rather than merely awkward and denigrating. Rock might have told the joke as a retort to the model minority myth.

Rock might have spoken to Asian American inbetweenness, pushed the Oscar audience to see beyond the threat of curve-raising automaton "tiger children" into a community made up of both math whizzes and sweatshop laborers. But then again, at this moment in history in that auditorium, before a nearly all-white audience that appreciated Black performance but rewarded only itself, while Asian Americans remained unrepresented and

African American solidarity under-reciprocated—maybe not. All things are not equal. Perhaps that kind of joke could have been told only in the context of a more equitable culture.

Throughout his career, the folklorist Alan Lomax argued for the importance of cultural equity. He said that arts produced by diverse groups of people are socially valuable because they offer us ideas, technologies, and values that help us figure out how to live together. The real benefit of a vital, equitable culture lies well beyond the money there is to be made. It offers us a sense of individual worth, bolsters our collective adaptability, and forms a foundation for social progress. In that sense, cultural diversity is just like biodiversity—at its best, it functions like a creative ecosystem. The final product of culture is not a commodity, it is society.

But we are far from that ideal. If cultural activism and justice movements can succeed in decentering whiteness and improving access and representation—and all the evidence suggests that the odds on that are still very long—we will still need to address the ways in which we see each other. Perhaps one day we may no longer need an #OscarsSoWhite hashtag. But we will still have to deal with the kinds of inequities that made #NotYourMule. What, then, will a culture of transformation look like?

VANILLA CITIES AND THEIR
CHOCOLATE SUBURBS

ON RESEGREGATION

I.

It was the mid-2000s and all the kids around the way were wearing impossibly huge glasses, sporting sun-bright colors, spitting thickets of new lingo that required slang dictionaries always under revision. The music had sped back up, the raps were complicated and goofy, the synth lines bouncy, the bass lines wobbly, and the vibe always energy-drink high. Turf dance battles were liable to break out anywhere—on a lawn in front of an East Oakland youth center or at the Powell Street cable-car turntable in San Francisco. The Hyphy movement brought pride of place back—in a major way, you could say—and once again it felt good to be from the "Yay Area," caught up in the extra-prolific silliness of it all, the whole world watching and scratching their heads, then going dumb too.

The Bay Area had long been a vortex of creativity, a place where turbulent minds could find each other and develop the kind of weird ideas that could surprise the world. The future was in the fringe, and the visible part of that fringe included circuit-board-crammed Silicon Valley garages, painted Mission District alleyways, and East Oakland streets where muscle-car sideshows might take over any time of the day. For a few ecstatic summers, it seemed natural that a lot of the left-field rap spiking the national Top 5–only airwaves—E-40's "Tell Me When to Go" or Keak da Sneak's "Super Hyphy"—had been beta tested on the streets of Oakland ("The Town" in local parlance) and San Francisco ("The City").

In actuality much of the music was being made deep in the cut, far away from the metro center, along a nowhere stretch of interstate highway heading out of the Bay between the suburbs of Vallejo and Fairfield. Both places were fading military outposts not known for much, certainly nothing like the Black Panthers, the Summer of Love, the White Night riots, the antiapartheid movement, or Occupy Oakland. They had not developed public scenes of their own—folks just weren't rolling like that near Six Flags Discovery Kingdom or the Jelly Belly factory.

But Hyphy permanently broadened the hip-hop map of the Bay. E-40 was rapping about how he was running "my region." Keak da Sneak shouted out Central Valley ethnoburbs like Stockton and Modesto, Sacramento hoods like Oak Park and Del Paso Heights, even foothill mall towns like Citrus Heights, two hours away from San Francisco's Fillmore District. The Yay Area now officially covered nine area codes and two metropolitan areas.

At about the same time, artists in San Francisco's Mission District were fighting what felt like a last stand. For decades, the neighborhood had been home to rough-and-tumble dive bars, late-night pupuserías and taquerías, edgy clubs, theaters, and bookstores, and a deeply influential pan-Latinx bohemia. By the end of the 1990s, though, it was losing all its spiky edges to a creeping—then surging—flood of new gold-rush tech workers.

In 2004, Richard Florida's influential book *The Rise of*

the Creative Class captured the zeitgeist for the George W. Bush housing-bubble boom. Cities were the future, he argued, especially cities that welcomed the diverse, artsy, highly educated workers who formed the "creative class" driving the knowledge industries. The as-yet-unwritten story would be about just how much diversity and art these cities would sacrifice in order to get to their bright creative futures.

Over the next decade, the Mission became the place where all the contradictions contained by Florida's thesis exploded. As the memory of the dot-com bubble faded, the Sand Hill Road venture capital tap flowed again and Web 2.0 hit its inflection point. At public bus stops, un-permitted luxury charter buses picked up workers bound for Google, Apple, and Facebook campuses thirty miles away in Silicon Valley's wealthy exurbs, disrupting daily transit schedules and outraging residents. On the soccer fields, techies flashing city orders purchased for a $27 fee tried to expel brown youths whose pickup games had been running for years. In under five years, at least one elementary school shifted from 70 percent Latino to 70 percent white. Residents were evicted to make way for the workers pouring into creative-economy jobs at Twitter, Spotify, Airbnb, and Dropbox, ready to pay steeply in-creased rents or make mortgage down payments in cash.

When in 2013 the famed artists René Yañez and Yolanda Lopez—Yañez had helped found Galería de la Raza as well as its famed Día de los Muertos parade and Lopez had created some of the most compelling art of the Chicano movement—were evicted from their apartment, artists gathered to raise funds to help them and to mourn what the city had become. In a widely circulated letter to Yañez, performance artist Guillermo Gómez-Peña raged:

It's like you once told me, "This city loves to preserve its murals and to evict its muralists." After all, it's not only the "criminals," the homeless and the gang-bangers who are being removed from the streets to make them acceptable for the new dot.com cadre. Along with them go the poets, the performance artists, the experimental musicians, the transvestites, the sex workers, the Latino families, the low-riders, the urban primitives, the punks and postfeminist radicals, and the very activists who used to protect us from the greedy landlords and politicians, only to be replaced by people who either look like art students and supermodels (but definitely aren't) or like they were just dropped by a UFO straight out of an LA or a Houston suburb, complete with their state-of-the-art gym gear, designer dogs, and customized baby strollers. It never ends. And soon, they will wake up to an ocean of sameness. What will San Francisco have to offer them then? Absolutamente nada!

But don't you worry Padrino. All the "creative cities" that have managed to successfully destroy and/or evict their working class have ultimately been condemned to doom.[1]

Cities are cauldrons of change, it's part of their very allure. The tech economy has turned "disruption" into a value, an unqualified good. Cities have also been havens for economic and cultural diversity, which at their best become the engines of dynamism. But these times beg the question of whether disruption and diversity are really compatible. They also force us to look beyond the boundaries of the city, into how entire regions are being reshaped into new geographies of inequality.

From 1997 to 2013, there were nearly 12,000 "no fault" evictions in San Francisco.[2] The median price of an apartment rental climbed to $3,023 per month, the highest in the country.[3] By basic housing standards, even a median San Francisco family could not live in a one-bedroom apartment in the Mission without being considered at severe risk for displacement.

In "The City," the Black population was decimated. In 1970, African Americans made up 62 percent of the population in the Fillmore, Western Addition, and Bayview/Hunter's Point neighborhoods, which comprised much of the Black community. Forty years later, they made up just 24 percent. The racial income gap in San Francisco County strained belief: the median white household brought home $104,364 per year, the median Black household $29,503.[4]

In 1963, on a visit through these neighborhoods, James Baldwin was surprised by the amount of anger he encountered among Black youths. Urban redevelopment plans had been drawn up for the Fillmore and the Western Addition, which would have resulted in the tearing down of hundreds of Victorian homes. He was moved to say, "Urban renewal is Negro removal."[5] Baldwin was prophetic. Amidst the new tech boom, the Western Addition was rebranded "NoPa," a hipsterized take on "north of the Panhandle," by giddy real-estate interests shrugging off the weight of history and the disappearance of the Black middle class.

Displacement has a domino effect. Those pushed from San Francisco had to move somewhere. Between 2000 and 2013, Oakland's median household income climbed by 36 percent to $54,394. In 2015 alone, Oakland became the hottest market in the country. Rental prices in Oakland surged 20 percent to become fifth highest in the nation, just behind Washington, D.C.[6] The *New York Times* commissioned travel reporters to hype The Town's "quirky, independent appeal" and "thrilling cultural heterogeneity," even as longtime working-class residents who had made its rep packed up and hit the I-80—north to Richmond and Vallejo and Fairfield, south to San Leandro and Hayward, east to Stockton and Antioch and Tracy.[7]

Central to the Bay Area's sense of itself—indeed, central to the pitch made by tech chiefs, politicians, and real-estate developers to lure talent here—were narratives about its "live and let live" countercultural tolerance, its proud claim to being the birthplace of American multiculturalism, its refined appreciation for all the things that make up the good life: art, education, natural beauty, and good food. But in late 2015, confrontations in Oakland between white transplants and longtime residents reached a critical point. They took the form of noise complaints: new neighbors literally did not want to hear from the old.

In September, the Oakland Police Department broke up a gathering of African drummers that had been meeting weekly at Lake Merritt for decades. In subsequent weeks, police were called upon to stop musicians from playing in a historic African cultural center and worshippers from singing in two West Oakland Black churches. Drummers, dancers, and church singers quickly joined the ranks of anti-displacement activists in loud musical protests at city hall. The Oakland Creative Neighborhoods Coalition brought together demands for affordable housing and sustainable development with demands for cultural equity. Its motto was #KeepOaklandCreative.

It mobilized activists to join Sunday services at the churches that had received noise complaints. "When we're talking about Black lives," one community leader said, "it's good to remember that Black noise matters, too."[8]

In the half century between Baldwin's visit and René Yañez's eviction, perhaps San Francisco's multiculturalist moment had been only a brief, enlightened interval between an era of segregation and one of resegregation, another lost utopia in a place known for cursed Kool-Aid visions. And yet the same pattern has held all across the country, from Seattle to Chicago to St. Louis to Miami to New York City. If segregation once kept communities of color locked into certain neighborhoods, a condition relieved by the all-too-ephemeral victories of civil rights revolution, then the post–civil rights era has been marked by an unmistakable lurch back to resegregation.

Our elementary and secondary schools, the front lines of demographic change, serve as a telling index. Public schools reached peak desegregation in 1989, the year of Spike and Chuck's fabled summer. But because of growing inequality, residential "preferences," and anti-desegregation campaigns, school segregation rates have since been surging back toward *Brown v. Board of Education* levels.

Those rates have especially accelerated since the turn of the millennium. From the 2000–01 to the 2013–14 school years, the number of public K-12 schools classified as high poverty and/or predominantly Black or Latino more than doubled. These schools, which account for almost one in six of all schools, offer fewer math, science, and college prep courses, and have higher rates of students being held back, suspended, or expelled. Only 8 percent of white students attend high-poverty schools, while 18 percent of Asians and 48 percent of Black and Latino students do.[9]

Eighty percent of Latino and 74 percent of Black K–12 students attend majority-nonwhite schools. But whites remain the most segregated racial group of all. The average white student attends a public school that is 75 percent white. That fact mirrors another: the average white lives in a neighborhood that is 77 percent white—a rate of racial isolation that is at least twice that of all other racial groups.[10] White flight is moving in two directions—to the "real America" exurban edge where big-box retail and brand-new "traditional" homes swallow fields of gold, and back toward the romance of the city, where wealth and youth conquer place and memory.

Scholars and pundits have labeled such changes "The Big Sort" or "The Great Inversion," careful, neutral terms that barely hint at the despair, conflict, and chaos that free-market forces and political acquiescence have wreaked on many Americans. Bill Bishop has argued that Americans are sorting themselves into new geographic alignments that will define political polarization in the coming decades. Alan Ehrenhalt describes how U.S. cities and suburbs are becoming more like Europe's, where wealth is in the metropolis and poverty surrounds it. But the reason sorting or inversion hasn't become a popular frame is because "gentrification" has become the major story of our time. This is the word that has captured urban rage over massive displacement—the affective fallout of root shock and cultural clash, as well as the class stakes of eviction and redevelopment.

And yet, gentrification offers a peculiarly small frame for trying to understand these paradigmatic shifts. When rents reach the tipping point, when old industrial buildings flip or are razed for flimsy new ones made of glass and chipboard, when poor residents have to leave, the gentrification narrative hits its limit. It has the odd, counterintuitive effect of privileging the narratives of those able to hang on in the changing city. But what of those who are displaced? Gentrification has no room for the question "Where did the displaced go?" Instead, the displaced join the disappeared.

By itself, gentrification can't explain the new geography of race that has emerged since the turn of the millennium. It has almost nothing to say about either Hyphy or Ferguson. Gentrification is key to understanding what happened to our cities at the turn of the millennium. But it is only half of the story. It is only the visible side of the larger problem: resegregation.

II.

Cities are becoming wealthier and whiter. Aging suburbs are becoming poorer and darker. Those suburbs are being abandoned, policed, and contained the way that communities of color in inner cities were for the past century. And all of these problems are interconnected: the fate of Sanford, Florida, where Trayvon Martin was killed, tells us about the fate of San Francisco; the fate of Brooklyn tells us about the fate of Ferguson. Nationally, we are witnessing a process that is reproducing racial inequality on a vast level.

And all of this matters because place still matters. Segregation is still linked to racial disparities of every kind. Where you live plays a significant role in the quality of food and the quality of education available to you, your ability to get a job, buy a home, and build wealth, the kind of health care you receive and how long you live, and whether you will have anything to pass on to the next generation.

Ferguson, Missouri—the tiny north St. Louis County suburb of 21,000—is one of those invisible places to which many of the displaced went. Its story was not unlike many other colorized suburbs. It had once been a "sundown town" where Blacks were not allowed after dark. Then in the last quarter of the twentieth century, an African American exodus from the city transformed St. Louis County. Between 1970 and 2010, Ferguson went from 1 percent to 67 percent Black. The story of how that came to be, the story of Ferguson itself—as community organizers there often note—reveals much about the America that has been hidden, and is central to understanding the conditions we all face right now.

The American metropolitan area had been designed with the preservation of whiteness in mind. Robert Moses's grand plans for New York City—for a Manhattan as a shining global center of wealth, literally purged of darkness and blight—were built on exclusion. But so was the rise of the modern American suburb, envisioned as a harbor from industry and "the dangerous classes," and all the clamor, filth, and social ills that accompanied them.[11]

Beginning in the late nineteenth century, developers tried to pitch upscale city dwellers on the appeal of suburbs by emphasizing how they combined urban convenience and rural predictability.[12] Stability and permanence, the urban historian Robert Fogelson argues, were key to this utopic in-between—no alarms and no surprises, no Blacks and no Chinese, either. It also neatly befit the forward-looking optimism of the American frontier mythology. If things got too crowded, too loud, too unsafe, or too unfamiliar, those who could afford to would simply set out again, as one journalist in the 1920s wrote, "toward that fringe of green that will always be the ideal setting for home."[13]

St. Louis City and its suburbs proved especially innovative in designing resegregation. Black organizing against these practices was no less so. Historically, the St. Louis metro area was both the central hub of a pro-slavery state and a crucial node between Mississippi and Louisiana in the south and Chicago in the north. Perhaps this tension—between the place's legacy of racial domination and its gateway location—fated it to play a central role in many a crucial national legal battle over segregation.

In 1916, as the Great Migration began, and just a year before the East St. Louis massacre left thousands of African Americans displaced and dozens more dead, St. Louis City's white residents voted to approve one of the nation's first housing segregation laws. The ordinance forbade anyone from living on a block occupied by more than 75 percent of the other race. The Supreme Court ruled such racial quotas unconstitutional in *Buchanan v. Warley* a year later.

But when African Americans sought judicial relief and the courts declared segregationist policies and practices illegal, new structures of inequality—what Paul Jargowsky called the "architecture of segregation"—were erected in their place. After *Buchanan v. Warley*, the powerful St. Louis Real Estate Exchange accelerated the use of restrictive covenants.

Historically, covenants had been used to restrict "undesirable activities," such as using a home for commerce or heavy manufacturing, or building homes of materials other than brick or stone.[14] But now they were used to re-strict "undesirable people" from purchasing or renting homes in many neighborhoods—in this case, "people of the Negro and Mongolian race."[15] Most Black St. Louisans thus lived in a narrow rectangle of downtown, between Cass and Chouteau Avenues from Grand Boulevard to the Mississippi River. City officials then began to label Black neighborhoods as full of "blight," a status that placed them in zones of redlining and disinvestment, and threat-ened their residents with abandonment or displacement.

After World War II, African Americans sought to move into covenanted St. Louis city neighborhoods. When white resident Louis Kraemer filed a suit to block the Shelleys, a Black couple, from moving into a house for which a racial covenant had been struck in 1911, the case went all the way to the Supreme Court. The Shelleys prevailed in 1948, when the court used the Fourteenth Amendment to declare that racial covenants could no longer be enforced. Soon, subsidized by post–World War II federal mortgage loans, whites began leaving the city for the county suburbs.[16] White flight and the politics of abandonment had begun.

The rise of St. Louis City had been premised on the idea that racial segregation was key to rising property val-ues. The rise of suburban St. Louis County rested on the same logic. Of 400,000 Federal Housing Administration mortgages guaranteed in greater St. Louis between 1962 and 1967, only 3 percent of city loans and less than 1 percent of county loans were given to African American families.[17] (In this regard, St. Louis was merely at the na-tional average.)

Government policies supported white mobility and suburban growth. They also enforced Black containment and accelerated urban decline. Federal public housing assistance incentivized the city to push Black poor into public housing downtown. Prospective Black homeowners continued to face steering practices that maintained a cordon around what real-estate agents explicitly called "the Negro community," which had been pushed north to the other side of Grand and Delmar Boulevards. This new physical border—between Black and white, poverty and wealth—would persist into the twenty-first century, becoming known as the Delmar Divide.

By the middle of the century, the downtown area had deteriorated so much that a visiting French corporate executive looked out from the windows of Monsanto's corporate headquarters and declared, "It looks like a European city bombed in the war."[18] City officials soon chose to clear the so-called blight. The razing of the Mill Creek Valley neighborhood in the 1950s displaced 20,000 African Americans.

At the same time, new industry, housing, and shopping popped up along the freshly paved interstate highways out of the city. Ferguson was a destination town back then, part of a ring of county suburbs that, historian Colin Gordon wrote, were helpfully rated for prospective white homeowners "according to average rents, population density, and 'the presence of Negroes.'"[19]

One of Ferguson's neighbors was Kinloch, known as "Missouri's first Black city," where Maxine Waters and Dick Gregory had been raised. In 1937, white residents in Kinloch failed in their political attempts to divide the school district to maintain school segregation, so they broke away to incorporate the new town of Berkeley. St. Louis County's home-rule laws allowed towns to propagate in this way, to allow whites to easily establish and protect their "fringe of green" from the crowded, the loud, the unsafe, and the unfamiliar. Eventually, ninety municipalities in all would be incorporated in St. Louis County.

In the mid-century, there was an explosion of new county towns, driven by a survival-of-the-fittest mentality. New towns built wealth, tax rolls, and city budgets, while reinforcing segregation and avoiding responsibility for the downward spiral of St. Louis City and the poorer county towns.[20] Gordon called this spate of town incorporations "a prolonged pattern of local piracy."[21] If the western vistas of Manifest Destiny were made possible by genocide, the picket fences of the Affluent Society were made possible by segregation.

"Fear—not forward-looking optimism—shaped the geography of metropolitan America," the scholar Thomas Sugrue wrote. "Sprawl is the geography of inequality."[22]

III.

In 1975, when Gerald Ford was running things in the West Wing and Obama was still a teen in Hawai'i, African Americans made up more than 70 percent of the population of Washington, D.C. "They still call it the White House," George Clinton joked in *Chocolate City,* "but that's a temporary condition, too." For a time, Parliament's tribute to "my piece of the rock" was not only funkily unavoidable, it was factually undeniable. And when Reagan took over the Oval Office, nearly 90 percent of the suburbs across the nation were white. It was no different in Washington, D.C. "Uh, Chocolate City is no dream," Clinton concluded. "God bless Chocolate City and its vanilla suburbs."

By the time the other Clintons—Bill, Hillary, and Chelsea—were moving into C.C. in 1993, suburbia had become more diverse, reflecting the removal of racial restrictions on housing, immigration, and jobs, and the subsequent growth of middle-class communities of color. Prince George's County, which stretches eastward beyond the District's borders, was majority nonwhite. In 2000, Montgomery County, north of the District, passed the same mark. By 2010, even Fairfax County, at its western and southern borders, was about a third nonwhite, the national average.

Many people of color moved to the suburbs for the same reasons that whites did—for more house, for comfort and convenience, for employment and educational opportunities. They also moved to specifically ethnic neighborhoods because a network of culturally welcoming neighbors and institutions had already been established. In some ways this trend reflected America at its best, the definition of the pursuit of happiness. But in other ways, it reflected resegregation's stark reality.

During the 1990s, many Black families left Washington, D.C., for Prince George's County. P.G.C. quickly became the highest-income majority-Black county in the country. *Washington Post* journalist Michael Fletcher described it as "a community that grew more upscale as it became more Black."[23] He and other *Post* reporters noted that in Fairwood, Prince George's richest neighborhood, the median household income was $173,000. But in the aftermath of the housing crisis, the county had the highest foreclosure rate in Maryland. Half of the loans made in 2006 and 2007 went bad.

Most of the blame pointed to the banks. Lenders disproportionately offered predatory subprime loans to Black buyers, even when by all fair lending standards they qualified for the very best terms.[24] Even if Prince George's County suburbs were high income, they too had been redlined by race.

It was this way all across the country. Neighborhoods where mostly people of color lived were more than twice as likely to have received subprime loans as mostly white neighborhoods. The foreclosure crisis revealed that high-income Blacks were not protected from racist and predatory housing and lending practices. Nor were Latino and Asian American home purchasers. So when the crash came, Blacks and Latinos were 70 percent more likely than whites to lose their homes to foreclosure.[25] A national study by demographers Matthew Hall, Kyle Crowder, and Amy Spring that examined nearly all foreclosures between 2005 and 2009 found unequivocally that "the highest rates of foreclosure were in racially integrated neighborhoods."[26]

Since the single biggest asset for an overwhelming majority of households of color was their home, the national wealth gap between whites and all other racial groups grew larger than ever. Between 2005 and 2009, white household net worth dropped by 16 percent, but plunged 53 percent for Blacks, 54 percent for Asians, and 66 percent for Latinos.[27] By 2013, the median white household held ten times the wealth of a Latino household and thirteen times the wealth of Black household.[28]

These impacts would have a long-term effect. One study found that before the Great Recession, white and Black households of comparable age, education, and median income were projected to reach parity in home equity by 2050. But in the wake of the crash, the study found white home equity would grow to over 1.6 times Black home equity in the same period.[29]

But there were other broad social impacts as well. De-segregated neighborhoods are the pathway to reducing precarity for households of color and increasing stability and sustainability for communities of color. But as demographers Hall, Crowder, and Spring wrote, "This pathway may have been significantly damaged during the foreclosure crisis, with housing distress piling up in these neighborhoods and white populations abandoning these areas at a quicker pace."[30]

Prince George's County's crisis played out against a tectonic demographic shift in Chocolate City itself. Sometime in early 2011, Washington, D.C.'s Black population dropped below 50 percent for the first time in over a half century. The non-Hispanic white population had grown by more than a third over the previous decade. During that time, one study found, Washington, D.C., had lost "virtually all of its low-cost housing in the private market," while the stock of high-end rentals nearly tripled.[31]

When beloved go-go bandleader Chuck Brown passed away in May of 2012, Black D.C. was stunned. Four generations of Chocolate City grew up with his music, a regionally distinct concert sound he had almost single-handedly created of funk, jazz, Afro-Cuban, and rhythm and blues. Among Brown's best-known sets was a genius medley of "Go-Go Swing" (a rewrite of D.C. native Duke Ellington's classic "It Don't Mean a Thing"), Lionel Hampton's "Midnight Sun," Eddie Jefferson's "Moody's Mood for Love," and the *Woody Woodpecker* theme, bridged by roaring percussive breaks during which he shouted out people in the audience by name and neigh-

borhood. In his later years, Brown mostly played in the
clubs of P.G.C., hollering the names of boondocks burbs
as much as the old Southeast and Northwest streets.

Brown was the beating heart of Chocolate City, and
when that heart stopped, people celebrated his life publicly with spontaneous block parties and joyful dancing that wouldn't stop. But the city had changed. The old
spots—a P.A. tape spot here, a BBQ spot there—seemed
to be disappearing. Million-dollar lofts were going up on
U Street. Underneath the grief over Chuck's passing was
a root-shock-level anxiety that a whole way of life might
have been passing.

IV.

During the 1990s and 2000s, many big cities actively de-
populated themselves of people of color and the poor.

They moved first to destroy the major housing projects
that had characterized the breakdown of the postwar
modernist dreams, the collapse of grand social engineering
into difficult and often dangerous realities. St. Louis, typically, had been among the first cities to act. The dramatic
1972 demolition of the Pruitt-Igoe projects eliminated
homes for 15,000, and evoked for many Black residents the
memory of Mill Creek Valley.

City leaders wanted to replace decaying low-income
housing with mixed-income housing. The idea was sound:
economic integration would give impoverished residents
better opportunities to succeed, and establish more diverse, stable communities. But its execution accelerated
resegregation. In 1992, Congress authorized the HOPE VI
program to facilitate this transition. Chicago destroyed its
Cabrini-Green and Robert Taylor Homes and used HOPE

VI funds to begin redevelopment. Similarly, San Francisco used HOPE VI funds to eliminate housing projects in the Mission and the Western Addition. But the replacement housing also reduced population density, exacerbating the shortage of affordable housing. Worse, only a portion of the new public housing went to old residents. The rest were forced to find affordable housing on their own. Many were scattered to the suburbs.

At the same time, development-minded city leaders pushed their police departments to focus on low-level "quality of life" crimes and nuisance abatement, while they also authorized all-out wars on drugs and gangs. Across the country, such politics led to urban policing driven by a sweep mentality, in which the poor, the jobless, the homeless and near-homeless, immigrants, and youths of color were criminalized, harassed, and arrested in their own neighborhoods. Routine brutality made victims of everyday people like Amadou Diallo and Abner Louima.

All the bodies swept up by these politics of containment had to go somewhere. So state and federal leaders authorized an explosion of prison building, infrastructure projects that largely escaped pork-barrel scrutiny. The declining suburbs and rural towns received their trickle-down. New carceral economies produced new relations of segregation, while the creative cities were cleared for gentrification.

V.

Since the 1970s, American neighborhoods have become dramatically segregated by income. A study of metropolitan areas with more than 500,000 people by Sean Reardon and Kendra Bischoff found that, in 1970, 17 percent of

Americans lived in the highest-income neighborhoods and 19 percent in the lowest. By 2012, those numbers had almost doubled—30 percent of U.S. families lived in the highest-income neighborhoods and another 30 percent lived in the lowest.

The latter number signaled especially troubling declines in opportunity, particularly for children living in the poorest neighborhoods. But Reardon and Bischoff argued that "the rising isolation of the affluent" also harmed the poor. "Segregation of affluence not only concentrates income and wealth in a small number of communities, but also concentrates capital and political power," they wrote. It also eroded "the social empathy that might lead to support for broader public investment in social programs to help the poor and the middle class."[32]

But even if the suburbs had been colorized, Blacks, Latinos, and Asians were more isolated from whites than they had been in the 1990s.[33] As demographer John Logan put it, "Suburban diversity does not mean that neighborhoods within suburbia are diverse."[34] The steep growth of Latino and Asian populations partly explained why. But white flight was the other key factor. In 2010, even low-income suburban whites lived in neighborhoods that were more than 69 percent white.[35] Blacks and Latinos were 40 percent more likely to live in more impoverished suburbs than whites.[36] Put another way, poor people of color tended to live in suburbs that were less white and more impoverished, while poor whites tended to live in suburbs that were more white and less impoverished. During the post–civil rights era, resegregation along both class and race lines intensified.

In the St. Louis metro area, where resegregation began almost as soon as desegregation efforts were successful,

African American precarity was not only economic. It extended from bodily safety to the community's very existence. "The starting place," the St. Louis writer and activist Jamala Rogers wrote in *Ferguson Is America: Roots of Rebellion*, "is making sure there's never any permanency in where Black people live."[37]

After the late 1960s, two legal cases accelerated the opening of St. Louis County to Blacks. In the first, an interracial couple tried to buy a home in Paddock Woods, an unincorporated area. When they were denied, they sued the developer. The Supreme Court ruled in favor of them in 1968's *Jones v. Mayer*, affirming the right to buy or rent a home without regard to race. Then in 1975, a court ordered Berkeley, Ferguson, and other nearby North County towns to desegregrate their schools. Black migration finally began to flow out of the city, west toward the Missouri River and north into the county.

But it did not get far. After school desegregation, white violence erupted. So many Black families along the North County racial border suffered vandalism, gunfire, and firebombings that they organized themselves into a group called People United for Home Protection, pressuring police to protect them and threatening to invoke the right to armed self-defense.[38] But policing—which had always been white—could also be too heavy-handed. As early as 1970, the U.S. Civil Rights Commission heard a Black resident in Kirkwood say, "I don't think there's a Black man in South St. Louis County that hasn't been stopped at least once if he's been here more than two weeks."[39]

Blacks were seen as movable and removable. City, county, and business leaders targeted Kinloch, the nearly all-Black town from which white residents had broken off to maintain segregated schools, for destruction to make way for the expansion of Lambert–St. Louis International Airport. Another historically Black town, Meacham Park, was annexed by its white neighbor, Kirkwood, then cleared for a Walmart complex. In Creve Coeur, authorities enforced code violations, denied building permits, and bought up lots to turn them into public parks in an effort to push out Black homeowners.[40] And when all else failed, whites fled deeper into the county.

By August 9, 2014, St. Louis County was more than 70 percent white and less than 24 percent Black. But one in four African Americans lived below the poverty line, more than double the ratio of whites. Most were concentrated in the North County. In Ferguson, three in ten neighborhoods had poverty rates of more than 40 percent.[41] Yet power in most of these municipalities remained in the hands of whites. They reorganized their entire systems of policy making, policing, and justice to exploit the poor, predominantly Black populations.

St. Louis remains one of the most hypersegregated regions in the country, alongside Baltimore, Cleveland, and Detroit—all key nodes on the map of the Movement for Black Lives. Of the fifty largest metropolitan areas in the country, St. Louis ranks forty-second in intergenerational economic mobility.[42] Resegregation matters because it pulls communities and regions downward, and because it impacts us not just right now, but the life chances of those not yet born.

And yet, too few of us were paying attention until Michael Brown was shot. In Ferguson, Black resistance revealed the structure of what America had become, and began to point toward new ways of envisioning our shared future.

HANDS UP

ON FERGUSON

Saturday, August 9, 2014. The area forecast had warned of storms, which might have brought small relief from the relentless heat, but as if in deference to the drama developing below the clouds, the lightning and thunder never came.

At a minute after noon, Michael Brown Jr. and his friend Dorian Johnson were stopped by Ferguson police officer Darren Wilson for jaywalking on Canfield Drive. Two minutes later, a resident of the Canfield Green apartments named Emanuel Freeman, under his handle @TheePharaoh, posted to Twitter: "I JUST SAW SOMEONE DIE OMFG." Then: "the police just shot someone dead in front of my crib yo." Through his balcony fence, Freeman took a photo of two policemen standing watch over Brown's lifeless body. With that image he posted the words "Fuckfuck fuck."

That started the flow of pictures, horrifying images traveling at tachyon speed over the Internet.

First, the young Black man, lying facedown on the boiling asphalt, head tilted to the left, left arm turned under him, right forearm with its "Big Mike" tattoo splayed away, blood from his head pooling and trailing down the pavement.

Then the picture of his stepfather, standing silent, defiant alongside a line of patrol cars holding a piece of cardboard on which he has scrawled: "FERGUSON POLICE JUST EXECUTED MY UNARMED SON!!!" And finally, the pictures of his mother in her unaccountable grief, asking the sky, "Why? Why did they do that?" These pictures were how millions who had not known him in life first came to know Michael Brown Jr.

Brown lay in the middle of a road that divided his apartment complex in half. Yellow tape was unfurled around the officer's SUV and the light posts, enclosing the young man's body and 800 square feet near the very center of the complex. Police cars filled the street in both directions.

People drew in. They congregated on the lawns and in the narrow shade of trees behind the police line— neighbors, family who knew him as Mike-Mike, friends who knew him as Big Mike, and many who didn't know him at all. Tweets cascaded in real time, pictures and videos taken from balconies and sidewalks, images and words trying to accrete into meaning.

Police placed orange cones near Brown's upturned baseball cap, bracelets, and stray slippers. But it would still be at least twenty minutes before they covered his body with a white cloth that was quickly stained red. As with Trayvon Martin's, Mike Brown's body was too big. His legs, bright yellow socks, and the Nike slippers that his companion Dorian Johnson had complimented him on just a couple of hours before, could not be contained by their cover.

TV cameras arrived. Witnesses—including Johnson— told reporters that Mike had had his hands up, but still the cop had shot him dead. Ninety minutes after the shooting, forensic detectives finally appeared.

Officers turned away Brown's uncles, his grand-mother, and his stepfather, Louis Head, from the young man's body. His mother, Lezley McSpadden, rushed down to Ferguson from her job in Clayton, and when she too was told she could not go to him, she paced along the border of yellow tape, holding her head and crying and cursing at the impassive cops. Ferguson Police Chief Thomas Jackson came and took McSpadden by the arm and walked her along the perimeter. The crowd surged and yelled epithets at the cops. She pleaded to the crowd, "All I want them to do is pick up my baby. Please move back."

Michael Brown Sr. arrived. He later wrote:

To this day, I don't know how or why I didn't explode into a murderous rage when cops held up their hands to stop me from getting to Mike.

"That's my son!" I screamed over and over, as if those words would mean something.

They didn't. I had to stand there like everyone else. . . . There I was, a semi-truck's length away from my son, seething with impotence and telling myself he wasn't really dead.[1]

By now, even the children had seen the body and blood of their neighbor and friend. Dozens more cops were assembling to secure the scene—a white police-man's killing of an unarmed young Black man—as if this street was theirs, as if the young man's body had never been anything but a mere stage prop in a performance of racial authority. None of these facts were lost on the crowd.

Some nodded in agreement when McSpadden gave an interview to a local television reporter. "You took my son away from me. You know how hard it was for me to get him to stay in school and graduate? You know how many Black men graduate?" she said, pausing a beat. "Not many! Because you bring them down to this type of level where they feel like, 'I don't got nothing to live for anyway, they gon' try to take me out *anyway.*'"[2]

People began chanting, "Kill the police!" Gunshots were heard nearby, and dozens more county and Ferguson cops—almost all white—were called. They arrived wearing bulletproof vests and brandishing assault rifles. They walked snarling police dogs up the driveways of the apartment complex, pushing people back toward their homes. In Canfield Green, Chief Jackson and St. Louis County Police Chief Jon Belmar's Ferguson resembled nothing so much as Bull Connor's Birmingham.

Smartphones and TV cameras were capturing all of it, and so, belatedly, the police tried to control the flow of images. They finally draped a long black cloth over Brown's body, and erected knee-high orange blinders. Later, officers were stationed in a circle around his body and told to hold up blue tarps as if they were curtains.

Hours after Brown was killed, his neighborhood resembled a war zone. On West Florissant, the street from which Brown and Johnson had been walking home, what residents would come to call "the tanks" made their first appearance. County tactical operations units deployed Lenco BearCat vehicles—vehicles designed for SWAT teams to use "in hostile Urban Environments," outfitted with half-inch-steel ballistic armor, two-and-a-half-inch-thick windows, and eleven gun ports, sold at a market price of $230,000 each.[3]

Through it all, Michael Brown's body lay under the burning sun like a provocation and a question mark. It would be more than four hours before his body was removed from the street. In the dimming daylight, firefighters hosed down the road and the policemen took down the yellow tape. The crowd followed Lezley McSpadden into the middle of Canfield Drive. Someone had given her a bouquet of roses. She removed the petals and gently dropped them to mark the spot where her son's blood still stained the road. People placed flowers and lit candles on the asphalt.

For Michael Brown's family, friends, and neighbors, and all those who had borne witness that day, time severed into a before and an after. August 9 would forever be Day One.

Elizabeth Vega, a Mexican American teaching artist and counselor, was in despair. She had been dismayed by the acquittal of George Zimmerman in the killing of Trayvon Martin the summer before, as well as by the recent shooting of John Crawford, who had been killed by police in a suburban Ohio Walmart while holding a toy BB gun that he intended to purchase. When she saw the pictures of Michael Brown's body, she called her friends and they decided to meet in Ferguson as soon as they could. In a tiny green 1991 Saturn loaded full of art supplies and water, Vega and two companions headed north out of St. Louis City.

There were two main approaches into Ferguson. One took you from the I-70 off-ramp through a lush gully in Jennings past Lutheran North High and the Norwood Hills Country Club. You turned left past the fifty-acre Buzz Westfall Plaza on the Boulevard, with its Target and Schnucks market, its Burger King, GameStop, T-Mobile, and U.S. Bank, all redone in New Urbanist brick and tan.

Then you drove down the hill on West Florissant, and when you crossed under the railroad tracks, you were in Ferguson.

Here the road narrowed and the buildings changed. On this side of the tracks, the mid-century buildings were low and worn, set back from the four-lane road with narrow parking lots. Beauty parlors, nail salons, boutiques, markets, storage lockers, and insurance brokers displayed modest window signs in neon and fluorescent. On August 9, the only buildings that broke the monotony were the McDonald's on the near side and the QuikTrip just past where Canfield Drive began.

At dusk, a full moon was rising, and three of the four lanes on West Florissant had become a parking lot of police vehicles bearing the names of more than twenty-nine departments from across the county. BearCat tanks moved up the fourth lane toward Canfield. Police in MARPAT camo battle dress awaited instructions in the parking lot of Original Red's BBQ next to the QuikTrip. Sirens lit the street in oscillations of blue and red. Helicopters buzzed above. Hundreds of Ferguson residents who had come down from their houses took in the scene with horror.

The other route into Ferguson began on South Florissant Road, running parallel to West Florissant, only two miles but a world away. Getting off the highway, you drove up its length through Cool Valley, past churches, gas stations, modest and tidy ranch homes, and the McCluer South-Berkeley High School, until you arrived in a tidy little business district where signs let you know you had arrived in Ferguson's historic downtown.

Above the strip malls, bars, and restaurants, the municipal compound containing the fire and police departments rose like twin headstones. The building that housed the Ferguson Police Department and Municipal Court was just completing a multimillion-dollar makeover, the most expensive city infrastructure investment in recent memory. When Vega heard West Florissant was closed, she drove up this route.

Across the street in the parking lot of Andy Wurm Tire & Wheel, several people were gathering, including Vega's friends from the Organization for Black Struggle, one of the area's oldest racial justice organizations. Olubukola "Bukky" Gbádégẹ̀sin, an art and art history professor at St. Louis University; her partner, Jonathan Fenderson, a professor from Washington University; and Montague Simmons, a former investment banker who now chaired the Organization for Black Struggle, were all there. Soon they were making signs and talking strategy about how to get answers from the police.

Vega spotted a young toddler who looked anxious, confused, and lost. She walked over to him, bent down, and asked the boy, "Baby, are you OK?"

He answered, "They shot Mike-Mike and I saw him dead in the street."

Vega took him and his six-year-old sister by the hand and said, "Come on, let's make a sign." As she took out the paper, the boy answered the question she was about to ask him—he had put his two small hands in the air. Together they traced his hands and arms onto the page and colored them in.

The group was now chanting, "No justice, no peace." Elizabeth asked the children if they knew what justice meant, and they talked about that for a bit. The girl decided she wanted to make a sign from the chant, so Elizabeth spelled out the words and she wrote the letters, drawing a backward *J*. These were not the kinds of things, Elizabeth thought, that white people in the county would ever have to talk to their children about.

The OBS members knew some of the demonstrators—local labor organizers, solidarity activists, anarchists. But as the crowd swelled, it looked less like an ordinary protest.

"We were on the sidewalk initially, and people would be driving by and honking in support. There were some people who slowed down and pulled over and asked, 'Why you all out here?' And somebody would talk and explain to them what had happened," Bukky Gbádégeşin recalled. "So many people pulled into the parking lot, and actually got out and started chanting with us."

"For us, that was unprecedented," said Montague Simmons. "The year before, [college honors student] Cary Ball Jr. had been shot twenty-some times [by St. Louis City police] and we may have been able to get thirty people at most."

Gbádégeşin said, "When we started [on August 9], we had about twenty, thirty people. By the time we finished [that night], it was like two hundred people, two hundred fifty."

The new demonstrators included mothers and grandmothers who had decided not to go home because they could not fathom the grief of laying their children down. They included young people like Tory Russell and Ashley Yates. Russell, a high school football coach and a day laborer, had left his house when he heard about Brown's death. He brought with him a group of people from Canfield Drive.

Yates and her girlfriend had come straight from her mall job in the ritzy Plaza Frontenac. Yates had pulled up

Black Twitter and her timeline was filled with the pictures. The two decided to head back across the county to where she had grown up. All of the protesters—old and young—felt as if they were being drawn into something bigger than themselves. As Elizabeth Vega put it, Michael Brown's killing was "the collective 'snap of the last straw.'"

As the evening of August 9 drew on, Ferguson police came out to ask who the leader of the protest was. By then, Yates recalled, "it was masses of people, so no one person could lead." But the crowd in the lot selected Russell and a small group of others to go inside to speak to the police. Meanwhile they held the signs they had made—"Mike Brown RIP," "Stop Cop Killing," "Police Brutality Has to End." They shouted, "Hey hey ho ho, killer cops have got to go." They adapted other chants from the sixties or Occupy Wall Street. But soon they were chanting a brand-new one: "Hands up! Don't shoot!"

Back on Canfield Drive, a Dumpster behind the apartments had been set on fire, and authorities quickly moved in. Lit by sirens, pushed back against the curb by growling police dogs straining at their leashes, residents and others who had earlier gathered around the scene of the crime were now surrounded by police on all sides. Near the lamppost that had marked the edge of the yellow tape line, they held their hands in the air. They too chanted, "Hands up! Don't shoot!"

One cop walked his dog over to the memorial that McSpadden had made for her son and let it pee on the flowers and candles. After the rest of the policemen got into their vehicles to leave, car by car they rolled over what was left of the memorial.[4] In the days to come, these memorials to Michael Brown Jr. would be destroyed over and over, as if to say, *This is the American way of remem-*

bering. But every time the memorials were torched or removed, people returned to put them up again. They had found the words to respond: *This time you will not get away with it.*

Later, many would debate whether Brown actually had his hands up when he was shot. Some pundits asking if the movement had been built on a lie. But that debate missed the point: the image resonated—and would continue to grow in the public imagination—because it captured a bigger truth, a deeper feeling. "Hands Up" was about the ways we saw race in post–civil rights America, and perhaps especially about what we refused to see—the blindnesses of a "post-racial" era. If, as intellectual Ruth Gilmore had written, racism was about the ways in which Blacks, whites, and others differently experienced "vulnerability to premature death," "Hands Up" was an argument for the right to live.[5]

And so began the daily protests in Ferguson against police brutality that continued unbroken for hundreds of days. It would become, as the Reverend Osagyefo Sekou said, "the longest rebellion in the history of the United States against police brutality."

Two weeks after Michael Brown was killed, the Arch City Defenders—a group of progressive St. Louis–area lawyers—released an influential white paper that exposed the link between policing, poverty, racial profiling, and city budget revenues.

Throughout the county, Blacks experienced stops, searches, and arrests at much higher rates than whites. Driving home while Black on a four-mile stretch through eight municipalities could be like running the gauntlet of gangs in *The Warriors*. For Ferguson, heavy policing was strategic. The Defenders report revealed that in 2013 the Ferguson court disposed of 24,352 warrants—more warrants than there were residents. Blacks, who made up 67 percent of the city and 6 percent of the police force, suffered 86 percent of traffic stops and 93 percent of arrests. Court fines and fees were the second-largest source of city revenue.[6]

A single violation—whether for a broken car taillight or failing to subscribe to the city's garbage collection service—could set off a cycle of disaster leading to eviction, loss of child custody, denial of loans and jobs, and even more jail time.[7] If one missed appearances or payments, not only might she face compounded fees and additional court fines, she might be arrested on the spot when she came to the court window to try to pay it off. The Defenders called it a "modern debtors' prison scheme."

A Department of Justice investigation launched after the protests over Michael Brown's killing found that Ferguson had implemented intentionally racist and unconstitutional practices in its policing and in its courts. Michael Brown and Dorian Johnson's jaywalking stop was not unusual. It was actually routine. "From 2011 to 2013," the DOJ noted, "African Americans accounted for 95 percent of Manner of Walking in Roadway charges, and 94 percent of all Failure to Comply charges."[8]

The DOJ also stated bluntly that "Ferguson's law enforcement practices are shaped by the City's focus on revenue rather than by public safety needs."[9] City officials pushed the police department to increase ticketing to meet budget projections. In turn, the department tied officer promotions to "productivity"; that is, the number of

citations an officer issued. In effect, this transactional approach coarsened the entire culture of Ferguson policing.

In one of its more stunning passages, the DOJ out-
lined how completely Ferguson's system dehumanized its
residents:

> Officers expect and demand compliance even when
> they lack legal authority. They are inclined to inter-
> pret the exercise of free-speech rights as unlawful
> disobedience, innocent movements as physical
> threats, indications of mental or physical illness as
> belligerence. Police supervisors and leadership do
> little to ensure that officers act in accordance with
> law and policy, and rarely respond meaningfully to
> civilian complaints of officer misconduct. The result
> is a pattern of stops without reasonable suspicion and
> arrests without probable cause in violation of the
> Fourth Amendment; infringement on free expres-
> sion, as well as retaliation for protected expression,
> in violation of the First Amendment; and excessive
> force in violation of the Fourth Amendment.[10]

Black residents of St. Louis County had long lived this.
"The trauma of it—this is something they've experienced
for years on end," said OBS leader Montague Simmons.
"This is their normal."

They remembered that early one morning in September 2009, during a heavy downpour, a welder named
Henry Davis had pulled his car over in Ferguson because
he couldn't see well enough to drive. The police officer
who arrived on the scene ran Davis's license plate, confused him with a man of the same name wanted for a

traffic warrant, cuffed him, and took him to jail. After the officer learned he had arrested the wrong man, he and three other cops reportedly beat Davis so severely they had to take him to the hospital. Davis was returned to jail, held for several days, and finally charged with "property damage" for bleeding on the cops' uniforms.[11]

They recalled that, in 2011, the Jennings Police Department—where Darren Wilson had begun his police career—had been disbanded and all its officers fired because of allegations of corruption and mistreatment of Black residents. When a mother and her child fled a traffic stop, an officer gave chase and fired shots at their car. A woman who had called to complain that her parked van had been damaged in a hit-and-run was beaten bloody on her porch after she made a joke about the van that the cop misunderstood.

Some still spoke of the 2000 Jack in the Box killings, in which two white undercover officers fired twenty-one shots into a car of two unarmed Black men, Ronald Beasley and Earl Murray, in the Berkeley fast-food franchise's parking lot. When community members criticized County Prosecutor Bob McCulloch for failing to indict the officers, he said of Beasley and Murray, "These guys were bums."[12]

Here were the strange fruits of resegregation: when August 9, 2014, came, one zip code in downtown St. Louis—where, seventy-five years before, African Americans had been confined in slum conditions and where, in 2013, police had shot Cary Ball Jr. twenty-five times—was among the fastest-gentrifying neighborhoods in the country.[13] But in North County, Ferguson—the once-invisible city transformed by Mike Brown's death into the new symbol of America's racial divide—would ensure that the trauma, hope, and humanity of the resegregated would no longer remain unseen.

Sunday, August 10: Day Two. Inside the Ferguson Police Department conference room, St. Louis County Police Chief Jon Belmar told reporters that Michael Brown had assaulted a police officer. He added that the officer had been placed on administrative leave, had been briefly interviewed Saturday, and would be interviewed again that day. He refused to give the officer's name and suggested that the Ferguson PD might actually return the officer to active duty. Outside, protesters could be heard chanting, "Don't shoot!"

St. Louis County and Ferguson police were withholding information, but on Twitter the hashtags #MikeBrown and #Ferguson had begun trending. It would not be until Friday that the world would know that the officer who had killed Michael Brown was named Darren Wilson.

Ashley Yates was in the crowd outside of the Ferguson Police Department. After protesting on Day One at the South Florissant headquarters, she had returned. She had recently graduated from the University of Missouri and was pursuing a career in fashion and design. But Michael Brown's death was leading her in a new direction.

Black clergy had come from their Sunday services to try to calm emotions, but Yates recalled that they were not finding much of an audience. She said, "People were rightfully angry." She found herself drawn to a Black female cop on the riot line. Yates asked her, "Don't you realize that if you have a son or daughter, or even you, you're just as susceptible?"

"These are my brothers," the officer replied. "If something happens, I know that every one of them is going to risk their life and shoot." But Yates challenged her: "No, that's the thing, though. They'll only protect you 'cause you're in blue." The policewoman refused to answer. Lines were beginning to be drawn.

Like Yates, Larry Fellows III was a young person interested in fashion and design. He had just moved into his first solo apartment in Carondelet Park with the money from his new health-care billing job. But the night before, as he and his friends celebrated with a housewarming, the party had been disrupted by the pictures. On Day Two, Fellows met his friends Johnetta Elzie and C. Jay Conrod at Canfield Green for an afternoon memorial. Afterward, the three split up to meet their families and planned to return with more friends for a sunset vigil that Brown's mother had called. But as evening drew near and they tried to return up West Florissant to Canfield, conditions had changed.

Thousands of demonstrators were in the streets, including mothers and children with hand-drawn signs that read "Honk for Mike" and "Enough Is Enough!" From a command post up the hill on the other side of the railroad tracks, in the parking lot of the Buzz Westfall Plaza on the Boulevard, armored Humvees and BearCat vehicles, riot-ready officers, canine units, and SWAT teams rolled down the hill into Ferguson.[14] They swept people back toward the QuikTrip. A low hum of panic was gathering.

"I'd never seen anything like that in my life. I was like, 'Why are they here?'" Fellows remembered. "Mind you, families and kids and people were coming out to pay respect to Mike's family, and to see all this intimidation by the police—it was frustrating. Because it was like, 'Didn't you take part in this murder? Then why are you here? You weren't invited.'"

Suddenly people were running toward them. "They're shooting!" a girl cried. Glass shattered to their left, and they turned to see youths looting the QuikTrip gas station. Inside, the employees gathered, put on jackets over their uniforms, and left through the back. After dark, fire engulfed the store.

The police had sealed off access to Canfield, so he and Elzie never made it to the vigil. Later, he grew outraged as he watched the newscasters focusing on the burned and looted QuikTrip and not on Michael Brown's murder, as if property were more important than people.

During the evening, as lines of cops and angry protesters stared each other down, some protesters, including Bukky Gbádégeşin, linked arms and stood between the two lines. She thought to herself, "I actually just don't want people to get hurt. I don't want something to break. I don't want the wrong store to be broken into that might trigger a police onslaught on everybody else."

Yet Gbádégeşin was deeply conflicted. "People were shouting, and really angry, with just a very nihilistic outlook, like, 'Why the fuck? Why can't we do this? If they're going to do whatever the hell they want, we can do whatever the fuck we want,'" she said.

The young radicals instinctively understood what the clergy and even seasoned radical organizers did not—that the aggressive police presence had already polarized the situation. Gbádégeşin and many others would quickly join the side of the young radicals, who were reminding the organizers of the limits of respectability politics. They were asking them, "Which side are you on? There is no in-between here."

After attending the sunset vigil, Ashley Yates tried to walk back up to her car on West Florissant. She began recording videos on her cell phone. At the QuikTrip, drivers gassed up their cars for free. People walked out with cases of drinks. Someone had spray-painted "Fuck 12" on the wall next to the door. Sam's Meat Market was being looted too. Against these scenes, she said the first thing that came to mind: "Los Angeles, 1992."

The cops stood in the middle of the street—some with dogs, many with their batons tucked under their arms and their gas masks on—simply watching as looters broke into stores. But at the same time, they warned Yates and others to stay on the sidewalk, between the police and the looters. The only things the cops seemed interested in protecting were the vehicles they had parked all along West Florissant. "They're letting everyone break into businesses," she said, "but they're keeping *us* out of the street."

Yates had parked her car up the hill near the command post, but the police had set up a barricade at Ferguson Avenue so that demonstrators could not march up there. They had effectively locked everyone in—demonstrators, looters, and residents. When Yates asked a white officer why she could not get to her car to leave, he told her, "You shouldn't have come down here. You should have known this was going to happen."

In the background, police dogs barked. Yates was astonished. She asked, "*Why* should I have known this was going to happen?"

"It's common sense," he answered. "You watch the news?"

She finally found a long path to her car around the police line. "They treat us like we ain't human," she said, as gunfire retorted in the background, "that's why they fuckin' rioting. I'm against this, man, but I *understand it.*"

After midnight, police fired tear gas volleys all along West Florissant to clear the area. The escalation had begun.

By Monday, Day Three, the canine units were gone, replaced with the heavy shit: snipers sitting atop armored vehicles equipped with ear-shattering acoustic riot-control devices; groups of paramilitary police toting tear gas launchers, fitted with fighting knives, training their night-vision goggles, their M4 carbines, and twelve-gauge shotguns on demonstrators. Ferguson looked like occupied territory, a zone of civil war. In one set of widely circulated images, a young dreadlocked man was walked back down a sidewalk by five gas-masked cops in full armor, their assault rifles drawn on him. He had his hands raised.

The young visual artist Damon Davis wondered if the police understood the optics they had created. "They got to know this don't look right," he thought to himself. He decided to head to Ferguson and found himself at the site of the burned-out QuikTrip.

There he found a block party going on. The QuikTrip had become a gathering place for the resistance, a temporary autonomous zone. People distributed water and food and made signs. Street-theater artists performed plays. Black Greeks stepped. Buddhist monks prayed. Punk bands played. B-boys rocked. The *Washington Post*'s Wesley Lowery wrote, "This was their Tahrir Square, their

Tiananmen Square. The place each night where they would make their stand."[15]

Davis recalled, "People was chatting, soapbox preacher dudes doing their thing. Everybody had a corner, and they got their own platform they're trying to get involved with. And then [over the police loudspeakers] they told everybody to leave."

Larry Fellows and Johnetta Elzie were in the street handing out water bottles, with Wesley Lowery standing alongside them documenting the scene, when police began firing tear gas canisters in high, smoking arcs into people's yards and at people's cars. Over the loudspeakers, the cops told people to go home. One of C. Jay's neighbors stood on her lawn and yelled back, "This *is* my home. *You're* the ones who need to go home." But the police marched forward through the red-and-blue haze toward the QuikTrip. Elzie felt something like a sudden sharp punch to her chest, and was breathless for a second. The advancing police had shot her with a nonlethal round.

On Wednesday night, Day Five, the street clashes reached a climax. Police were pelted with rocks, bottles, bricks, even Molotov cocktails. Robert Cohen snapped an iconic photo of Edward Crawford—dreadlocked and dressed in his favorite American-flag jersey, with a bag of Red Hot Riplets chips in one hand and a flaming tear gas canister in the other, poised to fling the canister back, away from the children with whom he had been marching.[16]

Cops fired stun grenades, beanbag rounds, Stinger balls that worked like flash-bangs, and PepperBalls— ammo that Fellows described as "weird Pokémon balls that spit out gas."[17] They arrested working journalists and St. Louis alderman Antonio French. The young protesters had come up with a new chant, "Unite, rebel, throw the guilty cops in jail. The whole damn system is guilty as hell."

The next morning, Attorney General Eric Holder, Missouri Senator Claire McCaskill, and other politicians, left and right, decried the police militarization. St. Louis Police Chief Samuel Dotson pulled his officers back from Ferguson, publicly denouncing the county police's war-like tactics. Even military personnel were outraged. When police pointed rifles at people's chests, one retired army officer told the *Washington Post*, "That's not controlling the crowd. That's intimidating them."[18] The journalist Radley Balko noted that the police seemed to have lost their mission: "The soldier's job is to annihilate a foreign enemy—it's to kill people and break things. A police officer's job is to keep the peace and to protect our constitutional rights."[19]

The same day, Governor Jay Nixon appointed Missouri Highway Patrol Captain Ron Johnson, an African American resident of Florissant, to lead the command. Johnson met with Michael Brown's family and marched with demonstrators. Thursday evening was the quietest of the week. But the authorities still had given no more information about the officer who had killed Michael Brown. In the community, there was a profound sense that police were protecting their own.

On Friday, Day Seven, at QuikTrip, Ferguson Police Chief Thomas Jackson held a press conference to announce that the name of the officer who had shot Michael Brown was Darren Wilson. But before he did, Jackson described Brown's August 9 robbery of Ferguson Market, which had immediately preceded his confrontation with Officer Wilson. Soon cable news channels were running the store's surveillance cam video of Brown grabbing cigarillos and pushing the Arab American owner as he walked out.

Why, asked reporter after reporter, did Jackson see fit to release the store video at the same time he named the officer? One of them read to the police chief a statement issued by the Brown family's attorneys: "Michael Brown's family is beyond outraged at the devious way the police chief has chosen to disseminate piecemeal information in a manner intended to assassinate the character of their son, following such a brutal assassination of his person in broad daylight."

Chief Jackson responded, "What I did was release the videotape to you because I had to. I've been sitting on it. Too many people put in FOI [Freedom of Information] requests for that thing and I had to release that tape to you."

That evening, the clashes resumed.

The images from Ferguson bolstered the protesters' argument that the most vulnerable lives were Black lives. "When an assault rifle is aimed at your face over nothing more than a refusal to move, you don't feel like the American experience is one that includes you," wrote rapper and Hands Up United cofounder Kareem "Tef Poe" Jackson in a letter to President Barack Obama. "We do not want to die."[20]

Ferguson was now *the* national story, and it had been largely shaped by the people and the protesters, not the police. The hashtag #Ferguson drove the story. By the end of Friday, the Pew Research Center found, more than 7.9 million tweets had been generated.[21] Social media fueled local and national interest, and organizing networks were forming. On the ground, many of the protesters were already getting themselves together. In the days that followed, Governor Nixon declared a state of emergency and called in the National Guard. But demonstrations continued daily from morning to night. "We got war enacted upon us," said Ashley Yates, "so people formed, basically, survival troops."

"You would go and be there all day," she said. "You'd move around, walk around, whatever, but those were the people you checked in with, those were the people who'd ask if you'd eaten, those were the folks you left with, who made sure you'd get home. That was an early form of organizing."

Yates and Fellows found themselves drifting away from their jobs and becoming immersed in a new daily routine of meetings, work sessions, and protests. Soon people were asking if their group had a name. When the two joined with Johnetta Elzie, Brittany Ferrell, Ashley Templeton, and others to call themselves Millennial Activists United, they were part of an emerging ecosystem of organizations led by young people, including Hands Up United, Young Activists United, Lost Voices, Tribe X, OurDestinySTL, and others.

"This is civil rights 2.0," said Damon Davis, who also found himself drawn into the fervent organizing. "It's not suits and ties anymore. It's tattoos and dreads and queer women of color out here."

Community meetings drew together over fifty different organizations to coordinate planning and training. In order to accommodate the needs of the growing movement, OBS brought in leaders and organizers from Oakland, Miami, Chicago, Los Angeles, and New York City. Between August and October, they trained over 200 organizers in nonviolent direct action, and hundreds more in areas such as emergency response, medical support, crowd control, communications, and de-escalation.

Montague Simmons of OBS said, "One of the things that falls real heavy on us when we hear it is that it's a leaderless movement. That's not true. We would say it's a leader-*full* movement."

Central to the new national resistance was an organization called Black Lives Matter that had been started by San Francisco Bay Area organizer Alicia Garza, Los Angeles artist and activist Patrisse Cullors, and New York/Phoenix–based organizer Opal Tometi. On August 10, as #Ferguson exploded on social media, so did #blacklivesmatter. What began as a social-media meme was transformed by the Ferguson uprising into a frame, a theory, and an aspiration for the emerging national movement.

The genesis of the idea had come the summer before, in the long hours of July 13, 2013, after the acquittal of George Zimmerman in the killing of Trayvon Martin. After the verdict was announced, Garza quickly posted to her Facebook page, "I can't breathe. NOT GUILTY." Her feed filled with posts from people who insisted they were not surprised. "That's a damn shame in itself," she responded. "I continue to be surprised at how little Black lives matter." She added, "Black people. I love you. I love us. Our lives matter."

Cullors's activism had sprung from the brutal beating of her brother by Los Angeles County jail officers. Garza worried too about her own brother, in whom she saw Trayvon Martin. The fragility of Black life was not the same as the fragility of white privilege. That night, the two women, who had known each other for years through organizing circles, talked for a long time about Zimmerman, Martin, their brothers, and what needed to happen next. Cullors put a hashtag in front of Garza's refrain and posted it to Facebook, and suddenly a big idea cohered. The next day, the two contacted Tometi, a friend and a communications expert, and a social-media campaign was born.

"Black Lives Matter" articulated an impatience with the politics of respectability. Proponents of respectability politics, Randall Kennedy wrote, "advocate taking care in presenting oneself publicly and desire strongly to avoid saying or doing anything that will reflect badly on Blacks, reinforce negative racial stereotypes, or needlessly alienate potential allies."[22] Such politics were resurgent during the Obama era. The president himself was both a source and a symbol of respectability politics.

But the Black Lives Matter activists were pro-queer feminists who worked with those on the margins of society: incarcerated people, domestic workers, and migrants. They thought of themselves as proudly, defiantly intersectional. They offered an expansive notion of what they called "Black love," a vision of radical diversity. Garza wrote,

> Black Lives Matter affirms the lives of Black queer and trans folks, disabled folks, Black undocumented folks, folks with [criminal] records, women and Black lives along the gender spectrum. It centers those that have been marginalized within Black liberation movements. It is a tactic to (re)build the Black liberation movement.[23]

Black Lives Matter challenged not only the content but the form of respectability politics—the traditional, charismatic Black messiah model that typically privileged straight male leadership and top-down, hierarchical infrastructures, such as those of the Black church. Instead, the movement drew on the methods and examples of Bayard Rustin, the gay man who had led the mobilization of the 1963 March on Washington while eschewing the spotlight; Ella Baker, the woman who had trained generations of organizers while strongly advocating modes of decentralized leadership; and Assata Shakur, the Black Panther activist exiled to Cuba who was still on the FBI's Most Wanted list and had written the lines they adopted as their mantra: "It is our duty to fight for our freedom. It is our duty to win. We must love each other and support each other. We have nothing to lose but our chains."

And they unapologetically centered Blackness, out of a historical and existential necessity. "We know that our destinies are intertwined," Garza wrote. "Non-Black oppressed people in this country are both impacted by racism and domination, and simultaneously, BENEFIT from anti-black racism. . . . When Black people cry out in defense of our lives, which are uniquely, systematically, and savagely targeted by the state, we are asking you, our family, to stand with us in affirming Black lives."[24]

Those who opposed the movement by arguing that "all lives matter" could not see the cold inhumanity of their stance. The systematic denigration of Black lives was inescapable, whether in shortened life expectancy or the growing list of extra judicial murders. In the United States, most conversations about race defaulted to a discussion about whiteness. But racism and inequality would never end if Blacks focused on easing white anxiety. Change would come only through a struggle to transform how everyone saw and treated Black lives. If Black lives mattered to all, then all lives really would matter.

By the end of August, a few weeks after Michael Brown's death, Cullors and Black queer feminist organizer Darnell Moore had organized a national freedom ride that brought 600 Black Lives Matter activists from across the country to join what people were now calling the movement in Ferguson. Organizers joined the daily protests on West and South Florissant and helped to stage other actions across the city. Activists from Palestine, Egypt, and Hong Kong tweeted words of support and practical advice, including how to deal effectively with tear gas.

The national network of organizations issued a set of demands, including the immediate arrest of Darren Wilson, the ending of police militarization, and reinvestment in resegregated impoverished communities. And to further these demands, organizers agreed to launch four days of civil disobedience they would call Ferguson October.

But as the start of protests neared, the area was shaken by three more officer-involved extrajudicial killings. The first—just three miles away from Canfield Green and less than two weeks after Michael Brown was killed—was captured on video. Police Chief Samuel Dotson told reporters that the suspect, Kajieme Powell, had raised his knife and that officers had shot him in self-defense. But the cell phone video he released the next day contradicted his own account.

Armed with nothing but a steak knife, Powell, a mentally ill man, had stolen two energy drinks from a store. He walked out, put the two cans down near the curb, and walked aimlessly in large circles, arguing with the young store clerk who had come out to reason with him. At that point, the man shooting the video thought the whole scene was funny.

But then the first police car arrived, and two officers—who would never be named publicly—emerged to tell Powell to put his hands up. Powell walked toward them, taunting, "Shoot me, motherfucker!" Then he started walking away from the police in another wide circle. When he came out of the loop to face the police, they fired twelve shots at him. He had not even drawn his knife. As the life bled out of Powell, one of the officers cuffed him while the other kept his gun trained on him.

On September 19, twenty-one-year-old Kimberlee Randle-King was arrested in Pagedale, a small North County town of cemeteries and an abandoned soap factory. She had been on her way to pick up her two children at her grandmother's house, but ended up in a group of people arguing and tussling on the street.

When she was taken in, police found Randle-King had seven "failure to appear" warrants for traffic and vehicle violations and prepared to take her back to a cell. The police report said that she "became 'hysterical' and claimed she would lose her 'job, house, and babies.' Kimberlee then said, 'I'm gonna die if I go back there.'"[25] A half hour later, Randle-King was found dead in her cell, hanging by her own red T-shirt.

Family and friends quickly gathered at the Pagedale jail in protest. They said she hadn't been anything close to suicidal. That case would soon find uncanny echoes in those of Sandra Bland and Kindra Chapman, and helped inspire a national campaign called #SayHerName that highlighted the impact of police brutality on African American women.

The last incident occurred on October 8, two days before the start of Ferguson October. When VonDerrit Myers and some friends emerged from a night market after buying sandwiches, an off-duty cop who was working a nighttime security job in his police uniform stopped them on a "pedestrian check." The cop identified at least one of the group as suspicious and carrying a weapon. Myers and his friends ran, and the cop gave chase before losing them.

Myers went up to his apartment to eat and put on a sweatshirt, then came back down to the street, where he encountered the cop again. What happened next remains a mystery. There were no official witnesses. But when it was all over, the cop had unloaded an entire clip, and Myers had been shot seven times in the back.

Police said Myers had been killed in a shootout and that there was gunshot residue on his hand to prove it. They noted Myers had been wearing a GPS ankle brace-let—a consequence of being out on bail for recent charges of unlawful use of a weapon and resisting arrest. The media was fed Instagram photos of Myers posing with guns.

But in the days that followed, the police modified their account of the night's events several times, talking of bushes that Myers had shot from that did not exist, and changing the make of the gun Myers supposedly carried. The officer, whose name would not be made public either, refused to be interviewed by a prosecutor.

Myers's family argued that a gun had been planted on him, and that he had been executed. The prosecutor agreed that the bullets fired at him could have explained the residue evidence, and Myers's DNA did not turn up on the gun that was found. Yet the prosecutor still decided not to take the case to the grand jury, stating that the evidence was inconclusive.

Perhaps Powell, Randle-King, and Myers did not appear to be as respectable victims as Brown. But then again, Ferguson police had tried hard with the store video release to make Brown appear not so respectable either. In the matter of Black lives, from Medgar Evers to the present, perhaps the perfect victim had never existed. Instead, there would be the stacked battle over sight and perception, the arduous struggle over the narratives made of complicated lives.

As Ashley Yates told Democracy Now!'s Amy Goodman, "Once we start realizing that we really are being weaponized—like our Black skin is being weaponized, people are seeing our melanin as a threat—then we can move forward."[26]

Ferguson October officially began on October 13.[27] In the dramatic week that followed, tens of thousands marched. Young Activists United occupied the St. Louis city hall rotunda. Bearing signs that said "Stop Killing Us" and chanting "Black lives matter," Millennial Activists United shut down the Plaza Frontenac. Protesters also closed Emerson Electric Corporation, and shut down two Walmarts and a Democratic Party fund-raiser. At the police station, dozens more were arrested, including Cornel West, the Reverend Osagyefo Sekou, and other religious leaders.

A student-led protest at St. Louis University led to a weeklong encampment by a group called Occupy SLU, resulting in a negotiated resolution called the Clock Tower Accords that committed the campus to more discussions about race, funding for Black student recruitment and retention, African American studies, a community center and community board committed to addressing inequality in the area, and a sculpture, designed by a Black artist, commemorating the encampment. Student organizer Romona Taylor Williams said, "We felt SLU needed to address some things related to inclusion. But this is not only about SLU. We need to occupy all of the institutions where there is systemic racism."[28]

Artists organized protests as well. On October 4, Elizabeth Vega, Sarah Griesbach, Derek Laney, and fifty other "Artivists" interrupted a St. Louis Symphony performance of Brahms's *Requiem*, standing throughout the Powell Hall to sing a version of "Which Side Are You On?"[29] The original song, written by Florence Reece for the bitterly fought 1930s Appalachian coal strike, included the words "They say in Harlan County there are no neutrals there." The Artivists changed the lyrics to "Justice for Mike Brown is justice for us all," and unfurled fifteen-foot-high banners painted by Jelani Brown that read "Rise Up and Join the Movement," "Racism Lives Here," and "Requiem for Mike Brown 1996–2014." Some in the overwhelmingly white crowd applauded, others could be heard retorting, "He's a thug." Most remained silent.

On one of the evenings, the Artivists carried a funeral casket to the front of the police line on South Florissant. The casket was covered in cracked, mirrored glass. The idea had come to artist De Andrea Nichols in a nightmare that she had one night after kneeling on West Florissant facing the tanks and the police with her hands in the air. At the head of the line, where protesters had been trying to break the police officers' impassive glares with questions and taunts, the sight of the coffin shook some of them. "Look into the mirror," one of the protesters told the police. "We are human too. You are not the only people who get to be human."[30]

As the St. Louis area girded for Prosecutor Bob McCulloch's announcement of the grand jury decision, Michael Brown's parents traveled to Geneva with a delegation of seventy Ferguson activists and human rights leaders. They testified before the United Nations Committee Against Torture. Back home, on a rainy Sunday, Tribe X, Missourians Organizing for Reform and Empowerment, and members of the Artivists staged a "die-in," lying down in the street to shut down traffic as other demonstrators chalked their bodies.[31] In the months to come, this form of protest became synonymous with the Black Lives Matter movement. Die-ins were staged in major shopping malls, transportation hubs like New York City's Grand Central Terminal, seventy medical schools, and on major arterial highways.

The next day, November 17, Missouri Governor Jay Nixon declared another state of emergency. Public schools in Ferguson and Jennings canceled classes. Police restocked tear gas, flex cuffs, and "less-lethal" munitions. The National Guard was placed on alert. Stores throughout the city and county boarded up their windows as if tornadoes were on the way. The grand jury announcement was still a week away, and already it felt like the worst hidden secret in Missouri was a coming nonindictment. Nixon had sent the message that riots were not just feared, they were expected.

In the tense days before McCulloch's announcement, local organizers and activists were assembling an infrastructure to support peaceful demonstrations and securing churches and community centers to serve as community sanctuaries and safe spaces. Damon Davis of the Artivists noticed that many of his friends were showing signs of stress and trauma. He wanted to create a work that would raise their morale, and lift up their message against the violence of the state and the media's anticipation of tear gas and fire. The result was a project he called *All Hands On Deck*.

Davis had been a hip-hop artist, graphic designer, and arts teacher. In 2014, he had won a public-art commission for a work that called attention to the Delmar Divide, the border between Black and white St. Louis, an enduring marker of the city's legacy of segregation. In the area north of Delmar Boulevard, residents were 99 percent Black, to the south they were 70 percent white. North of the Divide, the median home value was $70,000; south of it, $310,000.[32]

Davis proposed building a wall akin to the Wailing Wall in Jerusalem, where visitors folded written prayers into its cracks. In St. Louis, he said, people tended to speak bluntly about most things. "But Black and white people can't talk to each other here [about race]," he said. "The silence is even more deafening." He and his collaborator, Kevin McDermott, built a black wall that included slots for people to insert their notes and prayers.

After August 9, there had been a surge of letters. One read, "For Michael Brown and all the kids in Normandy and Ferg-Flor [Ferguson-Florrisant], I am so scared and so sad. I hope that those North of Delmar can get all the tools needed to talk to all those South of Delmar and West of St. Louis." Another read, "I am from the north of St. Louis. I am 17 years old. I feel like we live just like you just different neighborhoods."[33]

But then the responses trailed off. "I think nobody likes being uncomfortable, and I think real revolution takes everybody to be uncomfortable—the people up at the top, the people at the bottom." He added, "Most of this fight is mental, and I think the biggest weapon we have is the art that we produce."

Earlier in the fall, he had made black plywood arms and planted a field of them in a public park near McCulloch's house—symbols of the Hands Up movement rising from the grassroots. Now with the support of Global Grind's Michael Skolnik and the Artivists, Davis created fifty-one-inch-high posters of the hands of local Black and white organizers and activists—including Reverend Sekou, Tef Poe, Hands Up United's Tara Thompson and Abby Bobé, MoKaBe's Reeny Costello, an unidentified hacker from Anonymous, and Tory Russell's son, Lucas.

Davis had photographed their hands on white tables or against the snow. "Hands are what you do work with," he explained, "and this is what time it is: it's time for you to get up and help work on this if you want it to be any better." He then printed the hands in black ink on a blank white background. They seemed to attack the bland paternalism of Oliviero Toscani's 1990 Benetton ad featuring a black baby's hand in the palm of a white adult. But Davis had never seen Toscani's work. He simply favored the directness and simplicity of street art. "I really like stark contrast," he said. "And quite frankly, it is a very black-and-white issue."

Two days after Nixon's declaration, Davis, Skolnick, and a team of other artists-activists took the posters to the West Florissant businesses below the railroad tracks, whose windows had been covered with plywood as if in preparation for a hurricane. There they spoke to store owners and got permission to wheat-paste the broadsides on the boards. The state was preparing for a violent clampdown, an animus that would be confirmed by McCulloch's decision to announce the grand jury decision not to indict Officer Darren Wilson after dark, during the mid-evening hours when the August street clashes had usually begun.

But *All Hands On Deck* seemed instead to tap desires coursing across time and place—the 9,000-year-old black, red, white, yellow, and brown cave-art hand stencils at Patagonia's Cueva de las Manos that shouted, *We are here*; John Heartfield's street poster, *Five Fingers Has the Hand*, taunting the Nazi party from Berlin walls during the 1928 Weimar election season; even the gloved hands that John Carlos and Tommie Smith thrust into the air on the medal stand at the 1968 Olympics in Mexico City, their fingers closed into fists.

There were affirmation, defiance, and power here, but something else too—a radical vision of community. At the root of the preriot frenzy was the same kind of fear that had left Mike Brown dead in the street, that had driven a century of segregation and resegregation in the city and county. But these posters transformed the plywood from enclosing shields of fear into open walls that revealed the breadth of community—a child, a preacher, a barista, an activist, and others—in Black-and-white.

Their concert of raised hands suggested that on West Florissant, the young renegades, the small-business owners, and community members—perhaps even the police—were all linked together. Authority demanded submission. But when people raised their hands together, they might be demanding recognition, defying injustice, or even reveling in collective joy. Hands Up was the sharing of connection and communion, a possible ritual for de-escalation.

On November 24, St. Louis County Prosecutor Bob Mc-Culloch announced the grand jury's refusal to indict Officer Darren Wilson. In the long hours after the decision, the state and the media got exactly the clashes they wanted. Televisions ran hi-def split-screen images of President Barack Obama—once the embodiment of cultural desegregation and racial reconciliation—urging calm in the streets as police teargassed Black Lives Matter protesters on West and South Florissant.

In St. Louis City, organizers and activists were gathered at a bustling café at the edge of Tower Grove Park, not far from where VonDerrit Myers had been killed. Owned and run by a white radical named Mo Costello, MoKaBe's had long served as a gathering spot for activists from the Occupy, queer rights, and Black Lives Matter movements. White baristas often wore "Race Traitor" T-shirts and joked that it was their café uniform. Two weeks before, Mo had announced on Facebook that she would keep the spot open twenty-four hours a day for the activists. Pro-police activists flooded the cafés phone with calls and its Facebook page with comments, calling the coffee house "a business that supports cop killers."[34]

That night, the intersection at Grand and Arsenal in front of MoKaBe's filled with paramilitary police and armored vehicles. Police issued clearance orders while the crowd mocked them, "This is *not* an unlawful assembly.

You must disperse." Protesters backed onto the sidewalk and filled MoKaBe's. Dozens—including Amnesty International observers, parents, and children—were gathered inside, drinking steaming cups of free hot chocolate.

When windows were broken along Grand, police quickly moved to clear the corner. They fired rubber bullets at people on the sidewalk. Then they fired smoking tear gas canisters directly onto MoKaBe's patio and through the café's front door. Gas filled the interior, and dozens of stunned, choking, gagging patrons fled into the basement. As the stricken were treated with eye drops, riot cops marched behind the coffee house to fire more tear gas into the residential neighborhood to prevent patrons from leaving.[35]

After the smoke cleared, some ventured back out to yell at the police. But again cops gave a dispersal order, and from their armored vehicles dropped more tear gas canisters. St. Louis University professor and civil rights lawyer Brendan Roediger negotiated with the police for a way for the patrons to leave. Finally, they filed out of the café one by one with their hands up, and walked slowly away from the police line down the block to St. John's Episcopal Church. The next evening, police would return to form riot lines in front of the café.

Reverend Osagyefo Sekou had been at MoKaBe's on the morning of November 24 to attend an urgent meeting about preparations for the grand jury announcement. The young organizers had received him with a warmth and deference that they showed only a handful of other members of the clergy.

Back in the earliest days of the protests, mainstream clergy positioned themselves as brokers to the white elite. But when it became clear to the protesters that some of those same clergy were negotiating away their rights, they had chanted, "Fuck the clergy!" When the Reverends Al Sharpton and Jesse Jackson came to town, they received the cold shoulder from the street activists. In time, a popular T-shirt worn on West and South Florissant read, "Not Your Respectable Negro."

In October, at a massive interfaith gathering at St. Louis University's Chaifetz Arena, those same activists grew tired of the empty talk from church and civil rights leaders. They began chanting to let young people speak. When Tef Poe took the stage, they cheered. "For us this is not an academic issue," he told the leaders. "Y'all did not show up." He told them that he trusted the shirtless, bandanna'd boys and the young girls who had gone truant to be at the protests more than the elders. "This ain't your grandparents' civil rights movement," he cried. "Get off your ass and join us!"[36]

The small group of church leaders who had gained the respect of the protesters included the Reverend Tommie Pierson, who flung open the doors to his Greater St. Mark Family Church, less than a mile from Canfield Green, for demonstrators and community members, despite constant police raids; Renita Lamkin, the white pastor of St. John African Methodist Episcopal Church, who had been shot with a wooden baton round as she stood between advancing police and retreating protesters; Pastor Traci Blackmon of Christ the King United Church of Christ, who in rolling, sonorous, profound tones always seemed to capture exactly the words any crowd in a church or in the street needed to hear; and Reverend Starsky Wilson, who would move from marching in a hoodie to becoming the cochair of the governor's Ferguson Commission.

The young activists accepted Reverend Sekou as one of their own. He looked and talked like them. He was wiry and short, wore long dreadlocks and kept a rough beard, and he cursed like a hardcore rapper. He had been born in St. Louis, returned for high school north of the Delmar Divide, and had family in Ferguson and Berkeley.

Sekou was a third-generation Pentecostal preacher with an unusual pedigree. He had studied under Kwame Touré, who had given him his African name, and trained him to be ready for revolution. In his twenties he had been hired to teach teenagers at the Cochran Gardens housing projects and Stevens Middle School in St. Louis City, but he would say that he had studied under them too. From the teens, he learned that the hip-hop he had loved as a youth could catalyze consciousness in a new generation. In 2004, he became a key organizer for the National Hip-Hop Political Convention.

Ten years later, he was the formation and justice pastor of First Baptist Church in Jamaica Plain, Massachusetts, where he led a spoken-word and hip-hop ministry for queer youths of color. He was not easy on his peers and elders. It wasn't about age, he insisted, it was about attitude. "What do you fundamentally believe about young people?" he asked them. "Do you believe that they have value? Are you more concerned about their profanity than about the profane conditions that they live in?"

On the day Michael Brown was killed, Sekou was a scholar-in-residence at the Martin Luther King, Jr. Research and Education Institute at Stanford University, working on a book on the relevance of King's work to the present. When Sekou saw the news, he decided to come home. "I got on a plane on Thursday," he said, "and I flew back in time."

At Stanford, Sekou said, "I spent most of the time studying [King's] mistakes." He learned that when King came to Watts in 1965, he stepped off the plane and immediately spoke to reporters without having talked to anyone on the ground. When King finally made it across town to Watts, he was met by angry community members who had heard his press conference and chastised him for speaking out of turn.

Sekou decided that when he returned home, he would follow the lead of the twentysomethings, especially the queer Black women who were leading protesters to nonviolently face down the police and their firepower. He showed up and listened. He cooked meals for them and got arrested with them. In that way he earned their trust and became a target.

Four days after Governor Nixon declared a state of emergency, Sekou's house burned down under mysterious circumstances. At the same time, a letter circulated among the local clergy urging them to censure Sekou, accusing him of consorting with the likes of anarchists and refusing to condemn violence. In response, Sekou wrote his post–civil rights version of "Letter from a Birmingham Jail":

> I am a preacher of the gospel of Jesus—a poor dispossessed peasant whose life was cut short by state violence. For over a century, men and women in my family have preached that a hunted and hated people must always respond with dignity and deep abiding love. . . .

In August, when militarized police occupied Ferguson, Phil Agnew, co-founder of the Dream

Defenders, presented me with a challenge: "Ferguson will determine whether or not the church is still relevant." Our teargas summer has become a bitter winter of waiting, and the clergy seem to be running that risk of irrelevancy. . . .

Hence we are called to choose sides. Clergy must not only "support" protesters. We are called to be protesters—at once outraged and disciplined. By placing our bodies on the cross of a militarized police, deep infrastructural racial bias and a system that profits from human misery, a new way of being and seeing America and all its promise is being born. . . .

A willingness to be bruised, broken or detained for the sake of the gospel is our only option. Once we make this choice then and only then will our presence be warranted and blessed by the youth who quite reasonably distrust us. The side of love requires that we are uncomfortable.[37]

The piece was published on Sunday, November 23. The next night, after McCulloch's announcement, Sekou was back on West Florissant with his staff and a New York writer. Gunfire was erupting up and down the street. Buildings were on fire all around them. The police and their weaponry were on the move.

MSNBC had a compound on the street and had asked Sekou to come on the air, but they would not allow him to bring in his staff to safety. So he cursed them out and drove his staff across the street into a parking lot behind a chop suey, where they would try to wait out the running battles. After an hour or so, Sekou stepped out of the little station wagon to smoke a cigarette, and a police helicopter flew up and dropped a spotlight on him. He feared he might be killed in that instant. He walked away from his car, and strode quickly toward the police line.

"You better call off your boy," he yelled at the police lieutenant.

The cop laughed and said, "Oh, we like fucking with you, Rev." And the helicopter flew off.

The next night, when he heard that hundreds of police had again amassed at the corner of Grand and Arsenal in front of MoKaBe's, Sekou came to the café. He entered through the back alley the police had teargassed the night before, and when he came out to the front, he saw the riot police lines and hundreds of restless patrons on the patio. Police had already issued dispersal orders and seemed prepared to gas MoKaBe's again.

Sekou mounted a table and quieted the crowd. "My first thing is I need you to be safe," he said. "Do not engage them. Do not agitate them." He asked them to lock arms. He was improvising, he admitted, and a palliating laughter rippled through the crowd. And then Sekou took a leap of imagination or perhaps, he would say, of faith.

"We have already won," he said as he pointed back to the cops across the street. "They don't do *that* when we're losing. When they bring that out, that's because we've won already."

He remembered something the Occupy activist Lisa Fithian had taught him. He asked the crowd, "What does a heartbeat sound like?"

Someone said, "You mean the way it's going like boomboomboomboom right now?" The crowd roared.

"On a normal day!" Sekou said. "On a normal day, your heart goes . . ." And he hit his chest twice with his hand. He asked the crowd to unlock their arms and they joined him, pounding their hearts into a rhythm that could be heard across the street. The air itself seemed to change.

He turned to face the police now. "You are on the wrong side of history, and we have already won," he said to them. "We are peacefully gathered here in the tradition of Martin Luther King, Gandhi . . . This multiracial gathering is possible because of nonviolence. And that is the heartbeat of democracy that you hear.

"And so whoever your captain is, stand down. Go home," he said. "We'll be alright."[38]

The crowd laughed again. All along the police line, stiffened backs seemed to wilt. Then the cops turned to the left in file, turned again, and marched silently away down Grand Street.

Into the new year, a shocking but steady list of names filled the social media scrolls—Eric Garner, Tamir Rice, Rekia Boyd, Renisha McBride, Antonio Zambrano-Montes, Akai Gurley, Walter Scott, Freddie Gray, Laquan McDonald.

Deaths of people of color were nothing new. A Malcolm X Grassroots Movement report in 2012 had documented that every twenty-eight hours a Black person was killed by police, security guards, or vigilantes, "self-appointed enforcers of the law" protected by state codes like the stand-your-ground laws.[39] But with personal and surveillance technology and social media, Ferguson activists and the Movement for Black Lives now had the power to reveal what those statistics actually looked like.

As the winter drew on, the growing list sparked public mourning and rage, filling the streets and highways and train stations and bridges with protesters. A new song could be heard coming from the thousands of bodies in motion, written by Luke Nephew of the Peace Poets to memorialize Eric Garner and his last words:

> I still hear my brother crying, "I can't breathe"
> Now I'm in the struggle saying, "I can't leave"
> Calling out the violence of these racist police
> And we ain't gonna stop until the people are free . . .

Hundreds of Black congressional staffers staged a walkout in Washington, D.C., filling the steps of the Capitol with their hands up. Behind them, the Capitol dome was sheathed in scaffolding, a project still under construction and reconstruction.

"We vote, we don't get what we want. So poor people go out in the street, and we vote with our feet. We're tired of it," organizer Tory Russell told Amy Goodman. "President Obama, you must hear us. We're outside. Please have some sympathy for us."[40]

On December 1, the president met with seven young Black and Latino activists from Ferguson and New York, including Ashley Yates, to talk about policing. She mused that just months before, she had been folding clothes at Talbots in Plaza Frontenac. Now, on the anniversary of Rosa Parks refusing to give up her seat on a Montgomery bus, she was meeting the president to talk about race and policing.

The activists urged the president to demilitarize the police by ending the federal 1033 program that distributed surplus military equipment to local departments, to create a task force pushing for policing best practices, and to require the collection of data on police killings. They reminded him that police cameras did not prevent Eric Garner or John Crawford from being killed or denied justice.

Obama pivoted to talk about Black-on-Black crime, working hard, staying in school, and voting. He argued that he was proof that the system worked.[41] He urged them to decry the violence of the looters. But the activists insisted the overwhelming violence was being directed at them and their generation through what Phillip Agnew, executive director of the Dream Defenders, called "an investment and incentivizing of criminalization, of clamping down, of militarization, and police occupation and repression in our neighborhoods."

Yates added, "I wanna be able to refresh my browser 28 hours later and not see another headline that a black, unarmed citizen has been gunned down at the hands of those that are supposed to protect and serve us."[42]

Day 366. Sunday, August 9, 2015. At dawn on Canfield Drive, over a hundred people gathered for an interfaith prayer. When they arrived, the parking lots around the apartments at Canfield Green were quiet and nearly empty. The rebellion Sekou praised had now been going on for a year, had reached every corner of the country. On this ground history had been made, but the price had been dear. Dozens of families had left or been evicted.

Under the gray and coquelicot sky, pastors, rabbis, imams, ministers, residents, and visitors formed a large circle across Canfield Drive, the same circle that had been enclosed a year before by yellow tape. In the middle, the community's memorial to Michael Brown Jr. still stood. There people had placed teddy bears and other stuffed animals, flowers, candles, handwritten poems,

#UnitedWeFight postcards, stickers, roses, and daisies. They had decorated the orange police cones with "Copwatch" and "FCK12" stickers and the names of those shot by cops. Someone had left a single burned and tattered American flag where Michael had lain.

Together, those who had gathered joined hands and offered solemn prayers in the address of different faiths. Afterward, they drifted into small groups, some embracing, some talking, some meditating over the memorial. Then they went back to their cars to head to breakfast or to the business of the day's services. As the last of them lingered, the skies quickly darkened over Canfield Green. A loud rumble of thunder echoed over Ferguson and St. Louis, and down came a sudden, hard, blinding rain.

> *We will live on*
> *Forever and ever*
> —Flying Lotus, "The Protest"

Dorian Johnson woke up early in his Canfield Green apartment that Saturday. After getting breakfast for his girlfriend, he decided he needed some cigarillos to roll up some blunts. Down in the parking lot he saw his friend Big Mike helping an aunt get her kids into the car.

Dorian had met Mike Brown a few months earlier when another friend brought him over to play video games. Mike was quiet. "He don't like to talk to people," the friend told Dorian.[43] At six foot four and 300 pounds, Mike could seem intimidating. Dorian figured the silence was inhospitable—so he chatted Mike up. They found out they liked the same music—Drake, Kanye, Kendrick Lamar. Dorian, who was twenty-two, was impressed by the eighteen-year-old.[44]

"Everyone else's mentality be on some nonsense, silliness," he would say later. "But Mike had his mind set on more than that, helping others. I just got a good feeling from being around him."[45]

Dorian had a job, a girl, a new daughter to look after, wore his hair in dreadlocks, sported tats all over his wiry five-foot-seven frame, and was a regular at the basketball courts. Their friendship was young, and Dorian was the new guy in the apartment complex, but the kids looked up to Big Mike, and Mike looked up to Dorian.

Dorian had been through it. He had grown up on the north side of the Delmar Divide at the edge of St. Louis City, four miles from the Canfield Green apartments, in a neighborhood rougher than Ferguson. When he was a young teen, he stepped off the school bus into a gang shootout. A bullet caught him behind his knee. The incident scarred him physically and emotionally.

In 2010, he got his diploma and enrolled in Lincoln University, two hours away, in Jefferson City. It was a historically Black college, but Dorian came to feel that the campus police were treating him and other students from St. Louis differently from those from Atlanta or D.C., harassing him and making him frequently late for class.

Near the end of his freshman year, he was heading out to play basketball with some guys he knew when one of them stole a package. The police arrested the whole group and charged them all with misdemeanors, hoping one of them would snitch. When Dorian was asked to identify himself, he refused to give the policeman his name. Instead he just handed the officer his school and state IDs. Angered, the officer charged him with filing a false report. Soon Dorian quit Lincoln, moved back to St. Louis, and tried to get himself together.

But one day his brother lost control of the car he was racing. Dorian ran to the scene. The car had rammed into a tree and split in half. The police would not let him attend to his brother. He fought them so hard they handcuffed him and took him away. His brother was declared dead in the ambulance.

In time, the court date in Jefferson City had come and gone, and a bench warrant was issued for his arrest. One day, St. Louis County police stopped a car he was riding in, ran his name, and put him in jail. There he sat for two weeks until, as Wesley Lowery and Darryl Fears of the *Washington Post* reported, "St. Louis County police realized that Jefferson City police were not traveling 200 miles to get him."[46] That's when his luck turned. Dorian returned to face a Jefferson City judge, who threw out the false report charge and gave him probation.

Dorian descended the stairs to see Mike, who was wearing his red Cardinals cap, bright yellow socks decorated with marijuana leaves, and Nike slippers. Mike was staying with his grandmother at Canfield Green, where he had built a small studio to make beats. The two usually talked sports, clothes, fashion, and girls. But today Mike had trouble on his mind. The night before, he and another friend had stayed up talking about the existence of God and the problems they were facing. The friend said Mike was "going through a phase."[47]

Normandy High School was the third and last high school Mike had attended in four years. As Nikole Hannah-Jones reported, it was one of the poorest and most segregated in the state. It ranked last in academic performance, receiving from the Missouri Department of Elementary and Secondary Education a score of just 10 out of a possible 140 points for academic achievement, graduation rates, and college preparedness. Half the Black males never graduated.[48] Mike had not finished his credits when he posed for his graduation picture, but he was eager to finish, worked hard through the summer, and received his diploma on August 1, a proud moment for his family, especially his mother.

On Monday he would start attending Vatterott College, a for-profit vocational school that frequently advertised on late-night television. The college was partly owned by one of Mitt Romney's private-equity firms. It was known to federal investigators as a problem school whose business plan was built off student debt. Its former director of enrollment had pled guilty to federal financial aid fraud.

In an internal document prepared for its recruiters, the college pledged, "We Serve the UN-DER world Unemployed, Underpaid, Unsatisfied, Unskilled, Unprepared, Unsupported, Unmotivated, Unhappy, Underserved!"[49] Vatterott had lost a lawsuit brought by a former student, who, after taking out tens of thousands in loans, sought to recover fees for a diploma she deemed "worthless." A jury required the school pay her $13 million in punitive damages.[50]

Mike probably knew none of this. He was deeply worried about his future. Vatterott seemed like an opportunity to land a decent blue-collar job as an air-conditioning tech. In the old days, with luck, you might join a labor union and the middle class. Nowadays, there was no luck. You paid predatory schools for years for jobs they promised but probably would not get you.

In mid-July, Mike began going back to church. But he still brooded over his future. On the day they celebrated his high school graduation, he argued with his father. He announced he was becoming a rapper, but Michael Brown Sr. told him, "That's all fine and good, but you're gonna stay in school and you're gonna stay focused."

Mike responded angrily, "One day, the world is gonna know my name. I'll probably have to go away for a while, but I'm coming back to save my city."

Days later, on Tuesday, August 4, he spoke again with his father. His stepmother had just been diagnosed with chronic heart failure, just months after their house had burned to the ground. Mike said he thought she was going to die. Upset, his father hung up on him. Two days later Mike called another family member with a message for his father: "Pop's mad at me. Tell him I said what I said because I've been having these visions and images of death. Tell him I keep seeing bloody sheets."[51] He posted a cryptic message on his Facebook page: "If I leave this earth today, at least you'll know I care about others more than I cared about my damn self."[52]

Dorian could see Mike wanted to talk about life, so he told Mike about his experience at Lincoln, about the mistakes he had made when he was a freshman there. "I was telling him some challenges that he was going to face," Dorian later told the grand jury. "Basically our conversation was about future, future emphasis."[53]

The morning lengthened. Mike suggested the two of them go down to Ferguson Market. When they returned with cigarillos, they could roll some blunts and smoke together. They headed down to West Florissant.

They ran into two contractors who were laying down drainpipe. One of them had been digging, struck a tree root, and cursed. Mike talked them up. They spoke for a while, Mike talking about his anxieties and one of the contractors sharing his own. Mike told the man to ease up with his anger, that Jesus would help him through it. "Boy, you can grab a shovel and come down here and get to picking at these roots," the worker said. [54] Mike and Dorian laughed and left for Ferguson Market.

At the store, things got strange. Mike asked for a box of Swisher Sweets, and handed it to Dorian. Then he grabbed a smaller pack of single cigarillos, turned, and started for the door. The clerk ran to the door to stop him. Confused, Dorian put the box back on the counter and turned to see Mike shoving the clerk aside and walking out with the cigarillos.

Dorian followed Mike out onto West Florissant. "I looked at him, actually, looked at him for a while and stared at him because the times when I did meet him before that day, he didn't strike me as a person who would do anything like that," Dorian told the grand jury. "So I was asking him, I was like, you know, 'Hey, I don't do stuff like that. What's going on?'"[55]

Mike laughed and told him to be cool. Dorian knew they had been caught on camera, and when a police cruiser approached he started worrying. But it passed them by. There were no cars coming or going, so the two crossed into the middle of Canfield Drive to the median line—Dorian walking in front, Mike right behind. Mike was carrying half the cigarillos in each hand.

They picked up their conversation where it had left off. Dorian had a girl, a job, an apartment. How had he transformed himself? Mike wanted to know. How had he gotten himself on track?

"I knew he wasn't someone like me, I know he didn't grow up where I grew up from, where there was a bunch of violent gangs and violent stuff occurring all the time. I knew that much about [him] because I read from his demeanor he didn't come up that way," Dorian said. "I'm telling him about my life story and how I come up from a bunch of tragedies."[56]

What had been left unsaid? What else could he have told Mike? Questions were for the living, questions that could never be answered, but could never stop being asked.

Lives were complicated. The smallest things could trip you up. Those who could least afford it paid the most. Things could escalate in a heartbeat. The biggest mystery was how to turn it down without bowing down. And a life, in all its singularity and strangeness, was always worth the lifting, the telling, and the protecting, and never only for its fragility.

A couple-few cars passed them heading toward West Florissant. It was a Saturday in August, approaching high noon. They were almost home. A white Chevy Tahoe SUV marked "Ferguson Police" was just beyond the bend.

THE IN-BETWEENS

ON ASIAN AMERICANNESS

You went to college on the continent to become Asian American.

There were, as Jonathan Okamura once famously put it, no Asian Americans in Hawai'i. There were "Locals," there were Native Hawaiians, and there were *haoles*. Locals were the mostly nonwhite, often mixed-race sons and daughters who, during the early twentieth century, had forged a political and cultural identity oppositional to *haole* oligarchic rule. In that way, Native Hawaiians were always Locals. Locals weren't all Hawaiian. Some *haoles* were Locals. And if one had to ask, one wasn't a Local.

You were a Local. And by the time you were growing up in the spotless suburbs of east Honolulu, the *haoles* your age, especially the ones not descended from missionaries or politicians or profiteers, could call you "gook" and "chink" all they wanted, and it wasn't going to bother you. The words had no force, at least not in the way they might have to your parents or grandparents or great-grandparents. That was why *haole* kids had to push you around—to try to get you to pay attention.

You learned what it meant to be Asian American in Berkeley, California, where suddenly, significantly, you were a minority for the first time. When you rode home on your bike past the hippies in People's Park, they told you to go back where you came from. On a Saturday night, frat boys swarmed you and your Chinese American friend, got in your face, ping-ponged the both of you around their circle while simultaneously shouting, "Get off our corner" and "We love you little guys." You went with the homies to the Cineplex to see Brandon Lee kick ass in *Rapid Fire*, only to have an easy evening end with white guys in a pickup truck hollering, "Fuck off you fuckin' chinks." You went days and weeks feeling like you had never been seen. You were conspicuous and invisible at the same time.

This was hardly the kind of bullwhip-and-machete, chafed-hands-and-stooped-back racism your ancestors survived. You were not even sure you could call it racism. Maybe it had just been drugs or drunkenness or testosterone or you weren't raising your hand high enough. But still, your body was registering a kind of a system shock. You drank, got high, talked louder and with more false certainty, overcompensated.

When your *maoli* forebears landed in the islands there had been no others. And when your Chinese forebears landed in the islands, the Kingdom of Hawai'i allowed any immigrant who had lived there for a year to become naturalized. There were no restrictions on who could be a citizen. Exclusion was for other countries, like the United States.

Your high school teacher Mr. Lee taught you that Chinese people had built civilizations while Europeans were still messing around in loincloths. (He was also the school disciplinarian, so you got to know each other well.) But your folks didn't rule anything. They harvested rice and taro and watercress. They fought in boxing rings, delivered restaurant supplies, cooked for soldiers, fixed and maintained American military equipment. They gave their neighbors fruit from their land. They bartered in the markets for meat. They died by runaway plow or intended bullet, their hearts gave out or the water took them. They survived overseers, bosses, gangs, each other.

Hawai'i's statehood campaign emerged at the same time as the Southern civil rights movement. In 1959, they were given a choice to vote to make Hawai'i a state. Two generations before, they had not been given a ballot but the threat of bullets. But they chose to vote for it. Many Locals saw statehood as a culmination of a nonviolent revolution against *haole* minority rule, offering some as-yet-nameless reward. Not everyone did, though, especially Hawaiians who knew what had been taken.

You were born into the generation after that vote, around the time that Asian Americans announced themselves in San Francisco and Los Angeles and Boston and New York. It was long before "Asian American" had been reduced to a demographic category. Back then the term was still a courageous provocation, like a black leather jacket or a brown beret.

On the continent,.these angry young ones—most of them third-generation descendants of working-class East Asians—had invested in a Third World identity. They looked to anticolonial uprisings in Asia and Africa for inspiration. They spoke of revolution. They organized youths in Chinatown and Little Tokyo. They sold Mao's *Little Red Book* to the Black Panthers. They thought of Hawai'i the way some thought of the South or Aztlán, as a place where the answers were.

In 1980, Governor George Ariyoshi, the first Local Japanese man to rise to the highest post in the state, had given a soaring speech. In it he said,

It was here, in our red soil and black volcanic rock, that a new society was born. It was here that many from other societies gathered in disparate ways to start a new life and form a new society. It was here that sons and daughters of these early immigrants learned their lessons of tolerance and understanding and Americanism. It was here that they learned the verity that all men are truly created equal. . . . It was here that hard work and application were rewarded. This is the lesson of Hawai'i, and it is one that increasingly is being learned by the world.[1]

You didn't know yet of these words, but in the islands these ideas were natural as salt-soaked trade winds. As you became Asian American, you figured that you had an advantage over all your friends born on the continent, even those who had come from countries where whites were also a minority.

Your peers in college were struggling to figure out who they were. They had been especially hobbled by the violence of negation, external and internal, everyday and irruptive. Some of them had never met another Asian apart from their parents. Some of them had never really known white people, growing up in what the professors called "ethnic enclaves." All this was unfamiliar to you. But you were there with them in Asian American Studies 20A, everyone trying to figure out what they had in common with the person sitting next to them. Together you were going to learn how to be Asian American.

There was an instability at the heart of Asian Americanness. Panethnicity, you learned, was a creation of the state—a provocation turned census category. The state had been blunt and overbroad. It lumped all kinds of people of Asian and Pacific Islander descent together. It created new margins—if you were Filipino, Pacific Islander, South Asian, or Southeast Asian, were you really Asian? In classes, students debated fiercely: Did identity always need to be shaped from above? How can the object become the subject? Asian American Studies needed to constitute Asian American culture as much as it needed to describe it.

In your arrogance, your fury for living born of Local pride, ignorance, and insecurity, you had it all figured out already. You thought maybe you didn't even need the class, but for the fact that that's where the girls were. Your swagger was a gift of birth. You and your folks put Tabasco sauce in your saimin and ate your BBQ mix plate with chopsticks. You spoke your own pidgin: the sentences were structured as if spoken in Japanese, rich with loanwords from Hawaiian, Portuguese, Cantonese. You were a cultural chameleon, had spent a lifetime training in adaptation and code switching. Some days you probably felt like you came from superior stock. You wanted everyone, especially your Asian American friends, to come visit Hawai'i, see the proof.

Governor Ariyoshi gave that famous speech in 1980, during a period in which his government had come under fire from Filipino, Native Hawaiian, and Samoan activists who claimed that the state had discriminated against them in employment and educational opportunities.

The state administration was run predominantly by Local Japanese, Nisei who had come through the public schools at the height of the territorial Americanization campaigns. After World War II, this generation joined the

Democratic Party in large numbers, and became the vanguard of the multiracial working-class and nascent middle-class movements. This was where the idea of the Local had been forged—in multilingual labor meetings, on pidgin-chattering playgrounds, around luau tables, and at *kanikapila* jams. By the mid-1950s, the culturally Local majority—finding institutional expression in family associations, labor unions, the Democratic Party—had dislodged the *haole* Republican planter-oligarchy.

But two decades after statehood, Filipinos, Native Hawaiians, and Samoans were severely underrepresented in public jobs and disproportionately trapped in low-achieving public schools. Ariyoshi's speech had been delivered partly as a retort to those ethnic groups. It was a warning to wait their turn, because in Hawai'i we valued peace over justice, a peace that was ethnic in nature, and American in conception.

Jonathan Okamura's point was that Local identity had been forged in different circumstances than those that continental Asian Americans confronted. And the narrative of the Local—that the rest of the world was bigoted and racially divided, Hawai'i was the exception pointing to peace—blinded them to justice. How strong were these "lessons of tolerance," to have left the islands still so stratified?

But to Asian Americans on the continent, the idea of an identity forged in struggle—in epic labor uprisings on the plantations and in the shipyards and a rich hybrid culture birthed in work camps and schoolyards—was a powerful metaphor for their struggle against white racism. Building Asian Americanness was a bottom-up project of unity in diversity. But also, what could be more "e pluribus unum" than people from all these ancient warring cultures figuring out how to get along on American soil?

Some have portrayed the Asian American narrative—you have too—as a heroic one. But even as you tell this story, you wonder at the impossibility of Asian Americanness. There has been no Middle Passage to shape it, no common colonizers' language, except English, to express it. Sometimes you scroll through your Facebook page, and your Black or Chicano friends have posted a video or a quote or a news item of Black or Chicano folks doing something beautiful, ironic, or sad under the line "I love us." And it makes you think of your friend Eric Liu's question "Who is us?"

The category of Asian American sprawls: sixth-generation toddlers and undocumented teens; crazy-rich coeds chilling on Rodeo Drive or in Singapore Air first-class and couples on public assistance packing their meager belongings under eviction notices; architects and oncologists, nannies and bus drivers, seamstresses and factory bosses; class divisions that reflect the displacements of the Cold War and congressional preferences for the not so tired and not so poor; innumerable histories colliding, even in a single family. Yet here you are, the evidence of American warfare and familial risk and survival, making yourselves through panethnic coupling and an emergent culture of image, story, song, food. A tiger clan, a model fucking minority, a blueprint for multicultural democracy. You too are the exception and the exceptional. When you are summoned, you too may teach the rest of the world exactly how to get along.

You know there are white parents who are moving their children out of public schools that have "too many Asians." You know that pundits like Bill O'Reilly talk up

"Asian privilege" not out of concern for other people of color but because of a fear that whiteness itself might be eclipsed. What does it mean to be the evidence that racism is not real? To be fetishized by colorblind liberals and white supremacists alike? To be so innocuous that teachers and policemen and figures of authority mostly allow you the benefit of the doubt? To be desired for your fluid, exotic, futuristic, yielding difference? What does it mean to be the solution? For you, the Duboisian question is turned upside down. It haunts you.

Most of your life you have been in-between. The scholarship kid who wasn't a "hardship case" but still served your peers on the lunch line and wiped up after their cafeteria messes. The striver-class townie whose working-class grandparents lived in the country. The yellow face neither FOB nor ABC. The other nonwhite slamming in the mosh pit, cranking at the go-go, or getting down at the hip-hop jam.

You remember that children's rhyme. Actually, Rosie O'Donnell and Shaquille O'Neal reminded you:

Ching Chong Chinaman
Sitting on a fence
Trying to make a dollar
Out of fifteen cents

You remember trying to find your way between Black and white. You had taken every class you could with Ronald Takaki. He was the Seiji Ozawa of ethnic studies, a poof of white hair, a big laugh that shook his whole slender frame, an intensity that burned the sun. He had grown up not far from you, gone to the same school you did. His voice reminded you of your folks, their rainbow optimism and sugarcane pace. He joked about his surfing prowess and talked story like your uncles. He had been one of the first professors of Afro-American studies at UCLA. He taught you about slavery, slaughter, repression, the white imagination, the American mosaic. He gave you signposts, analogs, dots to connect.

You followed Ling-Chi Wang, bespectacled and serious, an authentic Chinatown renegade who, along with his barricade-storming comrades in arms, had stood up to the American war machine, the Six Companies, and the Kuomintang. He had the mind and the aloof mien of a master strategist. You drew close to him when he disclosed in a near whisper all the elaborate plots that the powerful had hatched to deny Asian Americans our basic rights. When he told you of how the university had implemented plans to deny Asian applicants admission in order to please its white alumni, you pictured yourself as a soldier in an important battle.

It's these battles that continue to unsettle you. Dr. Wang had exposed a national trend among elite universities to cap admissions of Asian American students, not unlike what they had done two generations before to Jewish American students. Every pronouncement Dr. Wang made—which you and your fellow student activists repeated with less care and precision but much more fervor—was about fighting discrimination against people of color, preserving both affirmative action and a meritocracy that was supposed to treat white and Asian applicants equally. Soon, Asian American students were organizing all across the country—at UCLA, Brown, Yale, Stanford, Michigan, and elsewhere. They were ambushing

college presidents with pickets, writing papers that de-
constructed the racial impact of admissions policies,
organizing community town hall meetings.

You have noticed that nowadays they don't teach this
history in Asian American Studies. It's not that heroic.

On matters of race, America teaches everyone to think
in binaries—zero or one, this or that. There is no in-
between. You know this, you refuse this, but you know
how hard it is to complicate a conversation the Other pre-
fers not to have.

You no longer believe in meritocracy. You believe now
that merit is never neutral—what really is?—and that the
rules are there mostly to preserve power. The right things
happen for the wrong reasons. There are no pure worlds.
There are only guiding values and the work of making
spaces and identities in common. But it was not easy to
learn this.

You thought it was a bougie Asian American thing to
be most upset not when the rules are stacked, but when
the rules are not followed. You mocked all the scare-quote
"activists" organizing their campaigns against racist
salespeople at the Acura dealer or "Ching-Chong" T-shirts
at Abercrombie & Fitch. They were sold a colorblind con-
sumer fantasy and they couldn't buy it. But you were the
one who got your peers to change the name of your student activist group from the Student Coalition on Asian
Admissions to the Student Coalition for Fair Admissions. And you wince now thinking about that, how fungible fairness is, how fungible bodies not yours are.

Back then, you thought anger was part of what it
meant to be Asian American. Still, at the community forums, you were stunned by the immigrant parents' rage.

How dare they ruin our American dreams? We have only tried to play by the rules. You feverishly joined the fight. You wrote op-eds, you lobbied powerful men. You helped drag the chancellor into a state senate meeting where he was forced to lose face. The administration undid all the little rule changes that had led to the steep drop in Asian admissions. They appointed a patient, empathetic Sansei man to implement a new process that might be more transparent and race neutral.

But success had opened the door to the conservative right. They believed that fighting over the rules—like showing how hundreds of Asian applicants were eliminated from consideration when the university doubled the weighting of SAT English scores—was sandbox stuff. So after the battle was won on campus, national anti–affirmative action activists flattened the nuances, turned up the binaries.

They said that good Americans were being hurt by so-called quotas. You knew that when they pointed to Asians, they really meant whites. But soon you saw Asians filing lawsuits from San Francisco to Boston to undo public school desegregation orders and consent decrees. You knew most of Asian America favored affirmative action and opportunity programs by more than two to one.[2] But you were also learning that well-funded right-wing institutions knew how to use quotas when it suited them.

Demagogues quickly followed, mobilizing white electorates. More often than they lost, they won. Magnet high schools and "highly selective" universities became more Asian, sometimes even more Asian than white, while numbers of Black, Latino, American Indian, and Southeast Asians admitted plunged. And twenty years later, whites were still three times as likely to be admitted to selective universities as Asians with a similar academic record.[3]

You felt dumb. You were the bougie Asian American. You were part of the ruination. You were Eldridge Cleaver's definition of the problem. Eventually you retreated, depressed and broken, from politics.

Gloria Anzaldúa, George Helm, and Jessica Hagedorn all realized that in-betweenness can create the stuff of epics. It is the mental geography through which we make the crossings that define us. It can also be a place of refuge. In Hawai'i, *pu'uhonua* were sites of mercy, where a warrior on the wrong side of the battle might find safety, where fugitives might find absolution. There, in between the space of the gods and the space of humans, they might rehabilitate and redeem themselves through moral, spiritual, and physical work. But these places were never meant to be places of permanent separation or disengagement. You did not go into a *pu'uhonua* to leave the world but to someday return to it. Unearned sanctuary is not a home.

These days, when demagogues talk about building walls, closing borders, checking papers, and sending people back where they came from, you think a lot about the story of Wong Kim Ark, a man who lived in between. He was born in 1873 and raised in the heart of San Francisco's Chinatown, long before it was a tourist curiosity, back when it was a segregated ghetto. In that era, Irish immigrant laborer Denis Kearney organized the Workingmen's Party of California, which blamed Chinese labor for stealing jobs from white workers. By 1882, Kearney had succeeded in getting Congress to pass the Chinese Exclusion Act.

Worried for their safety, Wong's family left after the Exclusion Act. But when he was seventeen, Wong decided to return to San Francisco, where he found work as a cook. In this way his story was like your own grandfather's, except that your grandfather's destination was Hawai'i. Wong returned again to China to marry and have a child and sailed back to the Bay Area in 1897. That's when he was detained. Wong was different from most other American-born Chinese only in that he decided to fight to have his citizenship recognized.

In the 1898 majority opinion, Supreme Court Justice Horace Gray wrote that the law was clear: "The [Fourteenth] Amendment, in clear words and in manifest intent, includes the children born, within the territory of the United States of all other persons, of whatever race or color, domiciled within the United States." The decision sealed the concept of birthright citizenship, an inextricable part of the foundation upon which present-day American diversity has been built. Indeed, its reliance upon the Fourteenth Amendment provided a perfect example of how the very idea of an immigrant or an Asian American is predicated upon the freedom struggle of African Americans.

The word "citizen" confers rights, rights that are invisible, that really appear only when they are denied. This is why Claudia Rankine has written of Blackness through the concept of "citizen," where the struggle to express the rights of citizenship too often outlives the body. You live in a racial state that formally denies difference, but in practice avows it, through the barrel of a gun or the conferring of papers.

The migrant is stateless, an embodied nowhere, a political nonbeing. But migration is what people do, on trains, as in Jacob Lawrence's great renderings, or on leaky boats or the undercarriages of buses you see in the flows of your nightly image stream. People migrate from hunger, war, poverty, hatred. They migrate because their homes have sunk, their homelands have been destroyed. They are no different from butterflies who migrate from the cold that would kill them. Sometimes, as with the Tohono O'odham, Apache, Yaqui, they become migrants because borders have crossed them. Sometimes they flee on rafts across the South China Sea, sometimes they die on rafts crossing the Mediterranean.

Migration is always a choice to live. The opposite of migration is not citizenship. It is containment, the condition of being unfree shared with all who are considered less than citizens. The migrant reminds the citizen of the rights that they should be guaranteed.

Nations are made of papers. Papers make the border. Papers also turn the migrant into the immigrant. The word "immigrant" is a formal legal term. It centers not the person, but the nation in which the person hopes to become a citizen. "Migration" centers bodies. "Immigration" centers bodies of law. The immigrant is therefore always troubled by the question of status: "legal" or "illegal." When the immigrant is between the migrant and the citizen, their freedom—and others' freedom, in turn—depends upon the answer.

How can a human being be illegal? Laws come from people. That is to say, they come from citizens. And yet what does it mean to be a citizen? Here you recall that there was a tragic coda to Wong Kim Ark's story. He had been declared a citizen at a time when the law denied the right of naturalization to Asians not born in the United States. Yet later in life, Wong migrated back to China, never to return. In other words, he did what all those casual racists told you that they wanted you to do, over and again— to go back where you came from, except of course, like you, Wong had not come from China.

What does it mean to be in-between? It means one can afford to sit on the fence, decide not to take a stand, to always reserve the privilege—while the battle rages all around—to disengage. Did Wong disengage? You cannot be sure.

You have never been one to sit on the fence. But you constantly worry about what it means to engage. You have learned that between intention and liberation, a lot, maybe everything, can go wrong.

Two decades after Wong Kim Ark's case was settled, two men of Asian descent petitioned to become citizens. Neither Takao Ozawa, a Japanese American, or Bhagat Singh Thind, a South Asian American, had been born in the United States. Yet Ozawa had lived in Hawai'i and graduated from high school in Berkeley. Thind lived and worked in San Francisco. Their status was "illegal." Both sought naturalization. They were also in-between. Each of them petitioned to have the Supreme Court make them citizens because they were not Black, and so, they argued, they deserved to be afforded the rights of whites.

Both of them lost. Until the 1965 Immigration and Nationality Act, all but a tiny number of men, women, and children like Wong, Ozawa, and Thind would be able to become "legal." These cases still trouble you.

You have said to Asian Americans that it's time to get off the fence. It's time to declare your Asian American-ness. But where will you all land?

The University of California at Irvine was the first university outside of Hawai'i to become majority Asian American. During the 1990s, Asians and Blacks in the segregated fraternity and sorority system enjoyed rich exchanges, and out of this ferment sprang many of the first Asian American choreo dance groups influenced by hip-hop and Black Greek stepping.

Then came the decadence. In 2013, a video of four frat brothers from Lambda Theta Delta, Irvine's oldest Asian American fraternity, surfaced on YouTube showing them lip-syncing to Justin Timberlake's "Suit & Tie." As it went viral, you and millions of others gaped in disbelief when a member came to mime Jay-Z's lines in blackface. At a place that seemed to have become the center, to borrow Long T. Bui's phrase, of Asian America's "model majority," the incident seemed proof that Asian Americans had just wanted to get down with Blackness until they could get up with whiteness.[4]

Late in 2014, Brooklyn rookie cop Peter Liang drew his gun while on a vertical patrol in an East New York housing project. He opened an eighth-floor door with the gun and, startled by a sound, fired a bullet into the unlit stairwell. It ricocheted and struck Akai Gurley, a young Black father, dead in the heart. Gurley had done nothing but decide not to take the elevator in the moment before Liang fired his gun. As Gurley lay bleeding to death, Liang offered no medical aid and fretted to his partner that he would lose his job.[5]

You had grown up around the Honolulu Police Department, where over the generations, the Queen's guardsmen and their descendants had gone to work. You knew what it meant to truly serve and protect. You had also lived, worked, and experienced enough in the hoods of Cali to learn exactly what it meant to exist in fear of the police. You were outraged at Liang's recklessness and heartlessness.

But when he was indicted, months after the officer who had strangled Eric Garner was let off, you watched as Chinese American protesters raised signs saying "Justice for Peter Liang! Stop Scapegoating!" You read in disbelief the words of a spokesperson for a supposed Asian American civil rights coalition that no one had ever heard of before: "If it was not for Ferguson and not for Staten Island, Peter Liang might not have been indicted."

Did they really believe the killing of Akai Gurley should be less indictable because it came at the hands of an Asian American officer? Were they really arguing that if hundreds of thousands of people had not taken to the streets in a freedom movement against state violence, this Chinese American police officer would have been afforded all the privileges offered a white cop who had taken the life of a Black person? If they thought Liang's indictment was unfair, the real question was still: Compared to what? They wanted Peter Liang to be seen as white, and Asian Americans to be afforded all the privileges of whiteness.

When Liang was convicted, they cried out again over the supposed injustice of it all. But when Liang was sentenced, by an Asian American judge no less, to five years' probation, they were silent. Maybe, you mused, their protests had worked. Or maybe, even if they had not protested, it still would have gone this way. Soon Ja Du, the Korean American shopkeeper whose 1991 killing of fifteen-year-old Latasha Harlins over a bottle of orange juice was fuel for the fire that became the Los Angeles riots, had also been sentenced to five years' probation. Like Liang, she never served a day in prison.

One night you are in a public panel discussion in San Francisco about the TV show *Fresh Off the Boat*, of all things, and you find yourself redirecting a question about whether Eddie Huang is guilty of cultural appropriation because of his use of hip-hop. The crowd has leaned in, because you are the Asian American face of hip-hop scholarship, or some such shit like that. And you catch yourself wanting to talk about how Asian Americans are guilty of much worse than rocking a backward snapback and above-the-knee shorts with sockless high-tops. Through their successful anti-desegregation lawsuits, they have made The City's premier high school 65 percent Asian, and destroyed equal opportunity for Blacks and Latinos. Asian Americans are the least segregated racial group in the region and in the country, and there are some in the community who would use that power to make things worse for other communities of color. But saying all this might not be wise. So instead you mumble something vague about resegregation in The City, and when the event is over you're still troubled. Why did you hold back?

An older Chinese American woman comes up to talk to you, practically runs up on you, and says she wants to ask what you meant by resegregation. She says that her husband is an activist, does great things for the community, and is a leader of the efforts to support Asian Americans in the public schools by getting rid of "quotas" for Blacks and Latinos. You're horrified. You tell her you disagree with her husband. As she stares at you, you hear yourself telling her that you don't believe he is doing anything to help Asian Americans.

"*I want to know what is wrong,*" she retorts, her eyes growing wide and her voice rising, "*with wanting to pro-tect our people from discrimination?*"

It's over. You want to walk away from her at this point. You want to walk away from being Asian American.

You know her story just by hearing her Sunset District accent, by seeing the stress lines on her face. You recognize this anger. All those times they were taunted, beaten, humiliated in the schoolyard or the street, all those people in authority who made them feel subhuman, all those jobs or homes they never got because of the color of their skin, all those times they played by the rules only to see a white person get ahead. You can feel her rage. Or rather, you think you can feel her rage. Maybe in this moment you're not really Asian American.

And now you should shut the fuck up and go home, but you can't. You tell her the days are over when Asian Americans should think only in terms of their self-interest, that Asian Americans ought to think about what it means to fight for justice and equity for all. You ask her, quite loudly and quite rhetorically, if she wants to defend a public school system in which the resources are allo-cated disproportionately to Asian Americans. Is that what she wants? Because if that's what she wants, that's not your idea of an equal and just society.

You feel good. You know you're right. Of course you're right.

Now she's shouting at you and people are staring. The crowd that has gathered looks at her with a bit of pity, not because they have any idea what the two of you have been arguing about, but because your provocations have made her emotional. That's when you finally walk away.

But later, when the night is over, you can't help but ask yourself: Who is the real Asian American here?

You went to college on the continent and became Asian American.

You tried it on like a suit and tie, or a suit of armor, and it fit OK. You got older and your body changed. It grew wings and calluses. The suit felt too tight. You left it in the closet and laced back up your Adidas.

You held close the ideals of your teachers and the people you admired—Grace Lee Boggs, Yuri Kochiyama, Fred Korematsu. But you worried that their names would sound dry on your lips, because you didn't have the words yet to say what you really wanted to say. You wanted an identity that would be not just a weapon but a tool, something that would not just bludgeon but build, that would not only justify your pain—inherited and accumulated—but let you stay open to the world, let you connect and grow.

You had children and they clarified you. Chinese, Filipino, and Hawaiian blood coursed through them. Things had not changed that much. They would still be seen as their grandparents and parents had been seen. But when you saw and heard your son stand in the spotlight before a mic telling audiences his family's stories, you knew that things had changed enough for them to know that their eyes were never too small, nor their noses too wide, their skin too brown, their bodies too weak, their minds incapable.

When you were their age, you weren't so sure. They had already surpassed the grand Asian Americanness of your youthful imagination. Now you hope they and their

peers are learning to see everyone in their full humanity—
their difference, their beauty, their glory; that they are
learning compassion and a sense of proportion, learning
to see beyond their own pain toward other people's suffering, toward the real justice they and those with whom
they share this vision might be able to create together.

You know now that there has to be an ethics of identity, an expansive, moral design to the way one lives.
When they choose to fight, because you know that someday they will have to, you hope it will not be merely for
greater numbers and more power if those numbers lead
away from equity, if that power is used to perpetuate injustice and inequality. You hope that they will know the
only thing worth fighting for, as Grace Lee Boggs taught
you, is to "create more human human beings and more
democratic institutions."

CONCLUSION

MAKING LEMONADE

When she first appears, we are not allowed to see her face.

We see her from the side, her arms draped over the roof of the SUV. She looks down, refusing our gaze. As she pushes back slowly, we anticipate seeing her but the shot quickly cuts to the side of a barn, a chain hanging heavily, a Southern tree. We are on the coast now, looking at the ruins of Fort Macomb, a brick bulwark wedged above the water to protect New Orleans from the British, taken by the Confederate Army in the Civil War, lost to the Union a year later, finally abandoned to storms and thieves. When we finally see her face she is below us, kneeling on a stage, her hair in a black wrap, her hands clasped as if in prayer, her eyes first closed then rising above us, as if pleading to a higher power. She wears a black hoodie.

This is the way Beyoncé's film for her album *Lemonade* begins—with a refusal. She denies us her gaze the way that her lover has denied his. Nicholas Mirzoeff, the scholar of visual culture, calls the look that two people share the most fundamental to humanity, "the look into someone else's eyes to express friendship, solidarity, or love." Through it, he says, "you, or your group, allow another to find you, and, in so doing, you find both the other and yourself."[1] Seeing each other fully and mutually is no less than the beginning of community. But *Lemonade* starts with a betrayal, the breakdown of this basic relationship. "Why can't you see me?" Beyoncé says later to her lover, repeating the line over and over. "Everyone else can."

Lemonade is a story of infidelity and promises broken, the journey of one Black woman from grief to redemption. When the album and its accompanying film arrived, they generated speculation about her supposed marital drama with Jay-Z. But in the manner of works like D'Angelo's *Black Messiah*, Kamasi Washington's *The Epic*, and Kendrick Lamar's *To Pimp a Butterfly*, *Lemonade* cannot be heard or seen separately from the exigency of the Movement for Black Lives.

In the way that post-hip-hop Black pop, like Malcolm X's oratory, has been about having conversations in public without compromise or apology, *Lemonade* is an album addressed to women and to Black people, but most especially to Black women. Her grief is connubial, lineal, racial. Her desire is to be seen not just by her lover but by *her folks*. The world can watch too because it might learn something. And in this way, her redemption rises from the personal to the social—not the *universal*, because we see each other from different vantage points of power, but that space where we come together, allowing us all to think about the ways we are broken and how we might mend the ways we break each other, how we might imagine healing, reimagine history, and dream freedom.

The film, codirected with Kahlil Joseph, sets these stakes immediately. We are placed in the South, a geography that looms large in the American imagination of slavery and segregation, life and death. We see Spanish moss on the trees, a camp of windowless shacks, young Black women dressed in white antebellum dresses. We linger on one woman in a shoulderless dress of gray and scarlet, a small tattoo below her neck reading "Dream Big ♥." Like the others, she stands silently as if bearing witness to the erased and untold history before them. "What are you hiding?" Beyoncé asks of her unfaithful.

"The past and the future merge to meet us here," she says. "What luck, what a fucking curse."

On the first song, "Pray You Catch Me," she is locked outside her lover's door, trying to listen in on his secret life, perhaps even seeking some kind of cathartic revelation of his crime. But she will not receive it. This moment is presented as stage one of her grief: intuition.[2] At the song's conclusion, she whispers desperately, "What are you doing, my love?" She has been alienated from her lover and herself. In the film, she removes her hood and flings herself off a building in a death dive.

Denial is the next stage. She tries to purify herself as if she were a Yoruba iyawo, reaching for a communion with higher spirits—wearing white, fasting, abstaining from sex and mirrors. But the pain is inescapable. She describes it by evoking the memory of slavery and its intimate relationship with religion—its rituals of sacrifice, self-flagellation, supplication, and suffering.

In "Hold Up," Beyoncé appears as Oshun, whom Joan Morgan writes is "the Yoruba Orisa/Goddess/Witch whose province includes affairs of the heart, (self) love, (re) birth, creativity, community, childbirth."[3] She rises from the river in gleeful catharsis, taking her "Hot Sauce" bat to muscle cars, store windows, and surveillance cameras. All around her explosions go off and the corner boys gape. "Tonight I'm fucking up all your shit, boy!" she taunts on "Don't Hurt Yourself." And yet Beyoncé is still reminding her lover that their fates are intertwined. She sings, "When you lie to me, you lie to yourself."

But after the release of anger, she descends into apathy and emptiness. She is broken and sleepless, even as she immerses herself in the daily grind and meaningless sex. She wanders through Southern mansions that do not feel like her own, that remind her only of what she has not gotten and who she is not. In "6 Inch," constant labor provides her with an escape and a mission—adding commas and decimals, stacking cash. But it is red-lit, exhausting, unsustainable. At the climax, the house goes up in flames.

Riots, we were reminded after Ferguson and Baltimore, are what Martin Luther King Jr. called "the language of the unheard." Here she stares back at us coldly, her face lit by the fire's flicker, obscured by the smoke. But as a sample of Isaac Hayes's version of "Walk On By" swells to its climax, she can be heard in a broken voice, crying out against her abandonment: "Come back."[4]

Yet there are also images of support and healing: women whose faces are drawn in Laolu Senbanjo's Yoruba-influenced body paint joyfully swaying together; Serena Williams twerking—respectability be damned— sharing the throne and a look of power with Bey; women whose long white dresses are tied together at their hands, moving like a pulsing heartbeat; Bey and her defiant sisters gathered around the SUV against which she had earlier hidden her face—its tires are gone and it's up on blocks, not going anywhere soon. Then the music suddenly drops out into a Malcolm X speech:

The most disrespected woman in America is the Black woman. The most unprotected woman in America is the Black woman. The most neglected person in America is the Black woman.

As he speaks, we see everyday Southern Black women of all ages—at the gas station, in their neighborhood, along a busy street. Their relaxed, smiling faces break up a narrative of pain. They seem to say, *We are here, we are surviving.* And the rest of us are reminded too of how unseen and unheard Black women can be.

Indeed, Beyoncé's method points to the way she wants her story to be read: as a larger, collective story of Black womanhood. The texts that glue the songs together in the film come from a collaboration with the Somali-British Muslim poet Warsan Shire. Much of the text comes from Shire's album *warsan versus melancholy (the seven stages of being lonely)*, which also traces the fall of a love affair.

She quotes Shire's poem "the unbearable weight of staying (the end of the relationship)" to reveal another layer of her own history: "i don't know when love became elusive / what i know is that no one i know has it." A New Orleans brass band gives way to Texas country blues on "Daddy Lessons," a musical nod to her roots. The lyrics of the song focus on her semi-estranged father, who left her family after he was discovered to have fathered two children outside of his marriage.

Beyoncé has to detach from herself, and slips into the second person as she thinks about her lover's refusal to reveal himself, and his refusal to see her. "Do his eyes close like doors? Are you a slave to the back of his head?" she asks. "Am I talking about your husband or your father?"

Through home video, father and daughter are shown in happier days—talking about seeing her grandparents, riding horses together. These are intercut with scenes of lightning storms, young girls playing, a teen donning her mother's pearls and examining herself in the mirror, a young woman being harassed on the street by a leering man, an ecstatic funeral march. Where is this search into her past heading? The care and protection of family is one possibility. The cycle of pain and revenge is another.

Her self-interrogation continues. "Why do you deny yourself heaven? Why are you afraid of love?" Love seems to be the most impossible option. We see her crying as she lies on the floor of the New Orleans Superdome. After the fires, this is the bottom. She has returned to the same place where she once short-circuited her Super Bowl half-time show, where eight years before, tens of thousands displaced by Hurricane Katrina, denigrated by the media, and treated as animals by federal and local authorities, sought refuge and comfort. On this Southern ground, she has seen the power and tragedy of humanity.

When the breakthrough comes, it happens in a kind of a baptism. We see her wading into the bayou waters at the head of a line of nine other women dressed in gauzy white Sunday dresses. Her moment of release comes when they look into the sun and raise their joined hands. She now has the power to break the curse, to return to her lover not as victim, but as redeemer.

At the March on Washington, King called on the nation to redeem its broken promises to African Americans. "Sandcastles" speaks of broken promises too. Her lover has broken his promise to be faithful to her. She has walked out on him and broken his heart. Yet she has also broken her promise to leave him. "Show me your scars and I won't walk away," she sings. He cannot walk away now. He must learn how to see her anew.

The climax of the film begins quietly—a gathering of beautiful young women for pictures and a feast. "So how we s'posed to lead our children into the future?" an elder asks. "Love." Then a procession of powerful images begins: young women holding pictures of men who may be their fathers or grandfathers; the mothers of the fallen—Sybrina Fulton, mother of Trayvon Martin; Gwen Carr, mother of Eric Garner; Lezley McSpadden, mother of Michael Brown—holding pictures of their sons.

As Camry Wilborn said of the scene, "For black women, even grief is political."[5] A young girl in a Mardi Gras Indian suit rattles her tambourine as she circles slowly round two empty dinner tables, a ritual to honor the ancestors. Finally, Beyoncé turns to Jay-Z's grandmother Ms. Hattie White, who is speaking at her ninetieth-birthday party, to reveal the importance of working to transform the sour into the sweet: "I was served lemons and I made lemonade." No set of images from Beyoncé—not even her standing in front of a screen that reads "Feminist"—better conjures a notion of Black women as bearers of legacy, protectors of justice, caretakers of boys, men, each other, than these.

Here is where we must make a leap—of faith, maturity, imagination—in the same way the post-Ferguson Movement for Black Lives has called on all of us to rethink everything from the bottom up—our shared language, images, and stories; the spaces where we learn, live, and work; who we think we are, individually and collectively. I use the term "we" here advisedly. If we are to undo resegregation and racialized exclusion, the fact is that some of us will have to work much harder than others. All of the forms of refusal, denial, and justification that preserve the structures of privilege will have to be undone to make room for those who are the most marginalized.

We often think of revolution as something to be won in bloodshed through war and the violent seizure of power. But as Grace Lee Boggs has put it, the next revolution might be better thought of as "advancing humankind to a new stage of consciousness, creativity, and social and political responsibility."[6] Her revolution would require us to move away from finding new ways to divide and rule, and instead move toward honoring and transforming ourselves and our relations to each other.

To be sure, Beyoncé's freedom dream is not about turning the other check. She riots through borders, breaks chains, "runs in truth." Her tears become flames. "I need freedom too," Beyoncé cries. But her freedom is not won in bitterness and revenge. Instead it is won through deep love. In the chorus of "Freedom," it almost sounds as if she were singing, "*Women* don't quit on themselves." In the end, they celebrate around the table with the gifts of the garden, the antidotes discovered in the kitchens of nurturance, the recipes passed down generation by generation.

The chorus of the album's penultimate song, "All Night," suggests that the prize of reconciliation is hot makeup sex. But the verses take the song in another direction. She becomes the light to her lover's darkness, a minister baptizing his tears. "Trade your broken wings for mine," she sings. "I've seen your scars and kissed your crime." In a line that has caused some consternation, Beyoncé sings,

> True love breathed salvation back into me
> With every tear came redemption
> And my torturer became a remedy

For some, this moment of transfiguration rings false. The discovery of infidelity, the baseball bat, the explosions— all of that feels more real. But it is also worth asking: What does it mean that we are better able to see pain than love? That rage and conflict in art are perceived as deeply felt, while reconciliation and joy are dismissed as mere sentiment? Does it reveal more about how broken we are than about the art itself?

She sings, "They say true love's the greatest weapon to win the war caused by pain." In granting redemption, she frees her oppressor. But forgiveness frees her too, allows her to heal from her trauma: the self-hatred, destructiveness, and suicidal depression. Her torturer is not *the* remedy, he's *a* remedy. As the song concludes in a bloom of strings, she whispers, "Oh I missed you my love." Of course she has missed her lover. But she has also found herself. The "my love" she names is also self-love. The writer Ijeoma Oluo has written, "*Lemonade* is about the love that black women have—the love that threatens to kill us, makes us crazy and makes us stronger than we should ever have to be."

Inspired by the Movement for Black Lives, the artist Carrie Mae Weems has recently turned her eye toward the notion of grace. She sees grace in the resolve of young Black protesters and the gentility of elderly Black women. Grace is the horizon of feeling that Kendrick Lamar describes when he raps in his verses of fighting and in his choruses of freedom.

"Grace implies freeing the bondage of the human spirit and suggests the breadth, scope, and depth of our humanity in the face of violence—acts that may be found in our everyday lives or reflected in public moments of collective grief," Weems has written. "Grace is meant to activate us, to propel us, to challenge us to see what we might prefer to remain unseen, and to act where we have been complacent and unable to move."[7]

Finding grace is an individual process that changes the social. It is about seeing each other in the world and seeing one's own place in the world anew. In that way grace can counter the lies, refusals, and aggressions that drive us toward segregation. We live in serious times, in which we need to be roused to the inequity in our neighborhoods, our schools, our metro areas, our justice system, our culture. Ending resegregation is about understanding the ways we allow ourselves to stop seeing the humanity of others. It is about learning again to look, and never stopping.

The film concludes with a tapestry of diverse couples in love and families at play. The South, which has been strip-mined for its real gothic horror, its brutal and violent racial ordering of life, its drama of division and death, has now transformed into a place of grace. As the Black feminist scholar Brittney Cooper put it, "[Beyoncé's] South is hot sauce, postbellum swag, and grandmothers who remind you that you gon' be alright." [8]

Yet it does not feel exactly like a happy ending. As Beyoncé wanders the ruins of the war fort in her *kente* dress, looking and singing directly to us, we wonder about her transformation. How easily could her newly won sense of self-love be undone? Did her lover deserve her generosity? Had she simply folded? Or is this indeed grace at work?

James Baldwin's most revolutionary and misunderstood idea, notes the intellectual Robin D. G. Kelley, was that love is agency. "For him it meant to love ourselves as black *people*; it meant making love the motivation for making revolution; it meant envisioning a society where everyone is embraced, where there is no oppression, where every life is valued—even those who may once have been our oppressors," Kelley wrote. This did not mean that Blacks should capitulate before whiteness and systemic racism, but exactly the opposite. He wrote, "To love all is to fight relentlessly to end exploitation and oppression everywhere, even on behalf of those who think they hate us."[9]

Each of us is left with the question: Can we, given all the pain that we have had inflicted upon us and that we have inflicted upon others, ever learn to see each other as lovers do, to find our way toward freedom for all?

The horizon toward which we move always recedes before us. The revolution is never complete. What we see now as solid and eternal may be disintegrating inward from our blind spots. All that signifies progress may in time be turned against us. But redemption is out there for us if we are always in the process of finding love and grace.

NOTES

INTRODUCTION: THE CRISIS CYCLE

1. Ruth Gilmore, *Golden Gulag: Prisons, Surplus, Crisis, and Opposition in Globalizing California* (California: University of California Press, 2007): 28.

2. East Asian American groups usually tend to fall between whites and other communities of color in all categories except educational attainment, income, and life expectancy, where they do slightly better than whites.

3. Lindsey Cook, "Why Black Americans Die Younger," *U.S. News and World Report,* January 5, 2015, http://www.usnews .com/news/blogs/data-mine/2015/01/05/black-americans-have -fewer-years-to-live-heres-why.

4. Anne Case and Angus Deaton, "Rising morbidity and mortality in midlife among white non-Hispanic Americans in the 21st century," *Proceedings of the National Academy of Sciences of the United States of America* 112, no. 49 (September 17, 2015): 15081.

5. David Graeber, "The Bully's Pulpit," *The Baffler* 28 (2015), http://thebaffler.com/salvos/bullys-pulpit.

6. Donald Trump, *Crippled America: How to Make America Great Again* (New York: Threshold, 2015).

7. Donald Trump with Tony Schwartz, *The Art of the Deal* (New York: Ballantine, 1987): 71–2.

8. Graeber, ibid.

9. Most districts were in Mississippi, Alabama, Georgia, and Louisiana. But districts in Arizona, Connecticut, and Utah also made the list. Nikole Hannah Jones notes that the official

U.S. Department of Justice list did not appear to be as up-to-date as the list that she and her team at ProPublica produced.

Nikole Hannah Jones, "Lack of Order: The Erosion of a Once-Great Force for Integration," *ProPublica*, May 1, 2014, https://www.propublica.org/article/lack-of-order-the-erosion -of-a-once-great-force-for-integration.

Department of Justice, "Educational Opportunities Section. Open Desegregation Case List," http://media.al.com/breaking /other/OpenCaseList%20byDistrict%20Public.pdf.

IS DIVERSITY FOR WHITE PEOPLE? ON FEARMONGERING, PICTURE TAKING, AND AVOIDANCE

1. Ryan Lizza, "The Duel," *New Yorker* (February 1, 2016): 38–39.

2. Donald Trump with Tony Schwartz, *The Art of the Deal* (New York: Ballantine, 1987): 53.

3. Paul Lewis, Maria L. La Ganga, Sabrina Sidiqui, and Nicky Woolf, "Donald Trump cements frontrunner status after big win in Nevada," *Guardian,* February 24, 2016, http://www .theguardian.com/us-news/2016/feb/23/donald-trump-wins -nevada-caucuses-results.

4. Lizza, ibid.

5. Tyler Cherry, "How Fox News' Primetime Lineup Demonized Black Lives Matter Protestors in 2015," *Media Matters for America,* December 29, 2015, http://mediamatters.org/blog /2015/12/29/how-fox-news-primetime-lineup-demonized-black -l/207637.

6. Alicia Garza, "A Herstory of the #BlackLivesMatter Movement," *The Feminist Wire,* October 7, 2014, http://www .thefeministwire.com/2014/10/blacklivesmatter-2.

7. Lorenzo Ferrigno, "Donald Trump: Boston beating is 'terrible,'" CNN.com, August 21, 2015, http://www.cnn.com/2015 /08/20/politics/donald-trump-immigration-boston-beating.

8. Inae Oh, "Trump Supporter Shouts for Black Lives Matter Protestor to Be Lit 'On Fire'," *Mother Jones,* December 15, 2015, http://www.motherjones.com/mojo/2015/12/donald -trump-black-lives-matter-protestor-light-on-fire.

9. Ali Vitali, "Trump 'Diversity Coalition' Holds Hectic First Meeting," *NBC News,* April 18, 2016, http://www.nbcnews.com/politics/2016-election/trump-diversity-coalition-holds-hectic-first-meeting-n557911.

10. Lisa Wade, "Doctoring Diversity: Race and Photoshop," *Sociological Images.* September 2, 2009, https://thesocietypages.org/socimages/2009/09/02/doctoring-diversity-race-and-photoshop.

11. Nancy Leong, "Racial Capitalism," Harvard Law Review 126, no. 8 (June 2013): 2154.

12. Tamara Winfrey Harris, "Black Like Who? Rachel Dolezal's Harmful Masquerade," *New York Times,* June 16, 2015, http://www.nytimes.com/2015/06/16/opinion/rachel-dolezals-harmful-masquerade.html.

13. Deena Prichep, "A Campus More Colorful Than Reality: Beware That College Brochure," NPR, December 29, 2013, http://www.npr.org/2013/12/29/257765543/a-campus-more-colorful-than-reality-beware-that-college-brochure.

14. Wade, ibid.

15. Terry H. Anderson, *The Pursuit of Fairness: A History of Affirmative Action* (New York: Oxford University Press, 2004): 14–15.

16. See especially Ira Katznelson, *When Affirmative Action Was White: An Untold History of Racial Inequality in Twentieth-Century America* (New York: W.W. Norton & Company, 2005).

17. Anderson, p. 82.

18. President Lyndon B. Johnson, "Commencement Address at Howard University: 'To Fulfill These Rights,'" June 4, 1965. Available online at the LBJ Presidential Library website: http://www.lbjlib.utexas.edu/johnson/archives.hom/speeches.hom/650604.asp.

19. Lisa M. Stulberg and Anthony S. Chen, "The Origins of Race-Conscious Affirmative Action in Undergraduate Admissions: A Comparative Analysis of Institutional Change in Higher Education," *Sociology of Education* 87, no. 1 (2013).

20. For a good discussion of the case of the University of Michigan, see Ellen Berrey's *The Enigma of Diversity* (Chicago: University of Chicago Press, 2015).

21. "Reparation, American Style," *New York Times*, June 19, 1977.

22. Emphasis added. University of California Regents v. Bakke, 438 U.S. 265 No. 76-811 (1978). Argued: October 12, 1977. Decided: June 28, 1979.

23. Terry H. Anderson, *The Pursuit of Fairness*, 158.

24. City of Richmond v. J. A. Croson Co., 488 U.S. 469 No. 87-988 (1989). Argued October 5, 1988. Decided January 23, 1989.

25. Ibid.

26. Parents Involved in Community Schools v. Seattle School District No. 1 Et. Al., 426 F. 3d 1162. No. 05-908. Argued December 4, 2006. Decided June 28, 2007.

27. Bakke, ibid.

28. Haeyoun Park, Josh Keller, and Josh Williams, "The Faces of American Power, Nearly as White as the Oscar Nominees," *New York Times*, February 26, 2016, http://www.nytimes.com/interactive/2016/02/26/us/race-of-american-power.html.

29. Esther Wang has written: "The writer Eula Biss posits that guilt is the dominant emotion of whiteness in the U.S., but I suspect that it's actually something else, and its core is something very different from guilt. Guilt implies a recognition of responsibility, culpability—knowing that you've violated some sort of unspoken social contract. The only social contract that exists in this country is this: You're supposed to know when it's OK to be racist, and when you have to hide it." Diversity fatigue is the weariness of having to hide it. On the other hand, what Wang calls "race fatigue" is the weariness people of color feel at having to negotiate double consciousness.

Esther Wang, "Watching And Reading About White People Having Sex Is My Escape," *BuzzFeed*, March 4, 2016, http://www.buzzfeed.com/estherwang/why-i-love-watching-and-reading-about-white-people-having-30#.uvjyawAkV.

30. Anna Holmes, "Has 'Diversity' Lost Its Meaning?" *New York Times Magazine*, October 27, 2015.

31. Claudia Goldin, Lawrence Katz, and Ilyana Kuziemko, "The Homecoming of American College Women: The Reversal of the College Gender Gap," National Bureau of Economic Re-

search, Working Paper 12139 (March 2006). Hannah Rosin, *The End of Men and the Rise of Women* (New York: Riverhead, 2012): 4.

32. Sean McElwee and Jesse Rhodes, "Young whites view race with rose-tinted glasses," *Al-Jazeera America,* January 18, 2016, http://america.aljazeera.com/opinions/2016/1/affirmative-action-remains-deeply-divisive.html.

33. Emphasis added. Academy of Motion Picture Arts and Sciences, "Academy Takes Historic Action To Increase Diversity," January 22, 2016, http://www.oscars.org/news/academy-takes-historic-action-increase-diversity.

WHAT A TIME TO BE ALIVE: ON STUDENT PROTEST

1. Dana Ford, "Meet the man whose hunger strike flipped the script at Mizzou," CNN.com, November 10, 2015, http://www.cnn.com/2015/11/09/us/jonathan-butler-hunger-strike-missouri-profile.

2. David A. French, "Missouri's Lesson: The Campus Wars Are About Power, Not Justice," *National Review,* November 9, 2015, http://www.nationalreview.com/article/426808/missouris-lesson-campus-wars-are-about-power-not-justice-david-french.

3. Thomas L. Friedman, "The Age of Protest," *New York Times,* January 13, 2016.

4. Jelani Cobb, "Race and the Free-Speech Diversion," *New Yorker,* November 10, 2015.

5. Mari Matsuda, "Public Response to Racist Speech: Considering the Victim's Story," *Michigan Law Review* 87, no. 8 (August 1989): 2322–23.

6. Martin Luther King, Jr., "Letter from a Birmingham Jail," April 16, 1963. Available online at: https://www.africa.upenn.edu/Articles_Gen/Letter_Birmingham.html.

7. Ebrahim Rasool, "Eyewitness Account: South Africa," Conference on Reconciliation and Change, Miami-Dade College, September 14, 2012. Transcript available at: http://www.cubastudygroup.org/index.cfm/files/serve?File_id=8c0fc23e-b32b-4a2b-afe4-858264e9a57e.

8. Martin Luther King, Jr., *Stride Toward Freedom: The Montgomery Story* (Boston: Beacon Press, 2010): 26–7.

9. These lists of demands have been collected at http://www.thedemands.org.

10. Leah Libresco, "Here Are The Demands From Students Protesting Racism At 51 Colleges," December 3, 2015, http://www.fivethirtyeight.com/features/here-are-the-demands-from-students-protesting-racism-at-51-colleges/.

11. Emma Pierson and Leah Pierson, "What Do Campus Protesters Really Want?" *New York Times*, December 9, 2015.

12. Sylvia Hurtado, "The Campus Racial Climate: Contexts of Conflict," *Journal of Higher Education* 63, no. 5 (September/October 1992): 539–41.

13. Robert Hughes, *The Culture of Complaint; The Fraying of America* (New York: Oxford University Press, 1993): 7.

14. Dinesh D'Souza, *Illiberal Education: The Politics of Race and Sex on Campus* (Free Press, 1991): 122–3.

15. Jack Stripling, "The Mount St. Mary's Presidency Was A Corporate Test Case. It Failed Miserably," *The Chronicle of Higher Education*, March 2, 2016.

16. Rankin & Associates, *University of California System: Campus Climate Project Final Report* (March 2014): vi.

17. Derald Wing Sue, Christina M. Capodilupo, Gina C. Torino, Jennifer M. Bucceri, Aisha M. B. Holder, Kevin L. Nadal, and Marta Esquilin.,"Racial Microaggressions in Everyday Life: Implications for Clinical Practice," *American Psychologist* (May-June 2007): 273.

18. Chester Pierce, "Offensive Mechanisms," *The Black Seventies*, ed. Floyd Barber. (Boston: Porter Sargent, 1970): 265–66.

19. The Microaggressions Project, "Guest Post 3: If these blogs could talk: characterizing power, privilege, and everyday life in the sciences," *Scientific American*, The Scicurious Brain blog, October 16, 2013, http://blogs.scientificamerican.com/scicurious-brain/guest-post-3-if-these-blogs-could-talk-characterizing-power-privilege-and-everyday-life-in-the-sciences.

20. American Dialect Society, "2015 Word of the Year is sin-

gular 'they'," January 8, 2016, http://www.americandialect.org
/2015-word-of-the-year-is-singular-they.

21. Greg E. Hill, "What's Next After the Protest?" Minority
Trailblazer podcast, December 15, 2015.

22. For a complete timeline of these events, see: Tessa
Weinberg and Taylor Blatchford, "A Historic Fall at MU," *The
Maneater* (2015). Accessible at: http://www.themaneater.com
/special-sections/mu-fall-2015.

THE ODDS: ON CULTURAL EQUITY

1. Marisa Kabas, "How Chris Rock's Oscars monologue
sparked the #NotYourMule protest," *Daily Dot*, February 29,
2016, http://www.dailydot.com/lifestyle/oscars-not-your-mule.

2. Academy of Motion Picture Arts and Sciences, "Academy
Takes Historic Action To Increase Diversity," January 22, 2016,
http://www.oscars.org/news/academy-takes-historic-action
-increase-diversity.

3. Chris Rock, "Chris Rock Pens Blistering Essay on Hollywood's Race Problem: 'It's a White Industry," *The Hollywood
Reporter*, December 3, 2014.

4. Kabas, *Daily Dot*, ibid.

5. Writers Guild of America, West, "WGAW 2015 TV Staffing Brief," March 2015, http://www.wga.org/uploadedFiles/who
_we_are/tvstaffingbrief2015.pdf.

6. Data is available at National Endowment for the Arts
website at: https://www.arts.gov/open-government/national
-endowment-arts-appropriations-history. Figures were adjusted
for inflation.

7. George Yudice, "The Privatization of Culture," *Social
Text* 59 (Summer 1999): 17–34. Also see: *The Expediency of Culture* (Durham, NC: Duke University Press, 2004).

8. Holly Sidford, "Fusing Arts, Culture and Social Change:
High Impact Strategies for Philanthropy," National Committee
for Responsive Philanthropy, October 2011, https://ncrp.org
/files/publications/Fusing_Arts_Culture_Social_Change.pdf.

9. Sidford, ibid.

10. Kory Grow, "Spike Lee Blasts Academy's Lack of Diversity in Oscar Speech," Rolling Stone.com, November 16, 2015, http://www.rollingstone.com/movies/news/spike-lee-blasts-academys-lack-of-diversity-in-oscar-speech-20151116.

11. Roger Schonfeld, Mariët Westermann, with Liam Sweeney, "The Andrew W. Mellon Foundation: Art Museum Staff Demographic Survey," July 28, 2015, https://mellon.org/media/filer_public/ba/99/ba99e53a-48d5-4038-80e1-66f9ba1c020e/awmf_museum_diversity_report_aamd_7-28-15.pdf.

12. Devos Institute of Arts Management at the University of Maryland, "Diversity in the Arts: The Past, Present, and Future of African American and Latino Museums, Dance Companies, and Theater Companies," September 2015, http://devosinstitute.umd.edu/What-We-Do/Services-For-Individuals/Research%20Initiatives/Diversity%20in%20the%20Arts.

13. Roger C. Schonfeld and Liam Sweeney, "Diversity in the New York City Department of Cultural Affairs Community," New York City Department of Cultural Affairs report, January 28, 2016.

14. Jose Antonio Vargas, "Here's what I've learned about #NotYourMule," Medium.com, March 1, 2016, https://medium.com/@joseiswriting/here-s-what-i-ve-learned-about-notyourmule-bfd0aa455d28#.n5vhkdd05.

VANILLA CITIES AND THEIR CHOCOLATE SUBURBS: ON RESEGREGATION

1. Guillermo Gómez-Peña, "A Heartfelt Letter to Rene Yanez & The SF Arts Community," Available at: https://docs.google.com/document/d/1pwjXeyT88TNdUgo8ZeNlBGAH-3GIKmloeLTqyxYVkm4/mobilebasic?pli=1.

2. All data from the Anti-Eviction Mapping Project, available at: http://www.antievictionmappingproject.net/combined.html

3. "The San Francisco Rent Explosion," Pricenomics blog, July 18, 2013, http://priceonomics.com/the-san-francisco-rent-explosion.

4. Joaquin Palomino, "Incomes Rise across S.F., except for African Americans." *San Francisco Chronicle*, October 3, 2015.

5. "Take This Hammer," KQED Documentary, 1963. Available at: https://vimeo.com/13175192.

6. Anna Marie Erwert, "Oakland: The nation's hottest rental market," SFGate.com, August 11, 2015.

7. David Farley, "In Oakland, Innovation Is On The Menu," *New York Times*, June 23, 2010. Freda Moon, "36 Hours In Oakland," *New York Times*, December 3, 2015.

8. Tulio Ospina, "Racially Profiled, Drummers Make Noise About Gentrification in Oakland," *Oakland Post*, October 2, 2015.

9. "High-poverty" schools are defined as schools in which 75 to 100 percent of students qualify for free or reduced-price school lunch. United States Governmental Accountability Office, "Report to Congressional Requesters: K-12 Education: Better Use of Information Could Help Agencies Identify Disparities and Address Racial Discrimination" (April 2016): 10, 59.

10. Gary Orfield, John Kucsera, and Genevieve Siegel-Hawley, *E Pluribus ... Separation: Deepening Double Segregation for More Students*, The Civil Rights Project/Proyecto Derechos Civiles (Los Angeles: UCLA, September 2012): 9–10.

See also Gary Orfield, *Reviving the Goal of an Integrated Society: A 21st Century Challenge,* The Civil Rights Project/ Proyecto Derechos Civiles (Los Angeles: UCLA, January 2009), http://civilrightsproject.ucla.edu/research/k-12-education /integration-and-diversity/reviving-the-goal-of-an-integrated -society-a-21st-century-challenge/orfield-reviving-the-goal -mlk-2009.pdf.

John Logan and Brian Stults, "Racial and Ethnic Separation In The Neighborhoods: Progress at a Standstill," Census Brief Prepared for Project US 2010, December 14, 2010.

11. Robert M. Fogelson, *Bourgeois Nightmares: Suburbia, 1870–1930* (New Haven: Yale University Press, 2005): 24.

12. Ibid.

13. Fogelson, pp. 30–31.

14. Fogelson, pp. 44–45.

15. Fogelson, p. 44. Colin Gordon, *Mapping Decline: St. Louis and the Fate of The American City* (Philadelphia: University of Pennsylvania Press, 2008: 83.

16. Gordon, pp. 96, 98–9.

17. Gordon, p. 96.

18. Robert Cantwell, "St. Louis Snaps Out of It," *Fortune*, July 1956, 120.

19. Gordon, p. 22.

20. Gordon, pp. 45–6.

21. Gordon, p. 45.

22. Thomas Sugrue, "The Geography of Fear," *Nation*, February 9, 2006, http://www.thenation.com/article/geography -fear/

23. Michael Fletcher, "A Shattered Foundation," *Washington Post*, January 24, 2015. Available at: http://www .washingtonpost.com/sf/investigative/2015/01/24/the-american -dream-shatters-in-prince-georges-county.

24. Ibid.

25. Renae Merle, "Minorities hit harder by foreclosure crisis," *Washington Post*, June 29, 2010.

26. Matthew Hall, Kyle Crowder, and Amy Spring, "Neighborhood Foreclosures, Racial/Ethnic Transitions, and Residential Segregation," *American Sociological Review* 80, no. 3 (June 2015): 542.

27. Rakesh Kochhar, Richard Fry, and Paul Taylor, "Wealth Gaps Rise to Record Highs Between Whites, Blacks and Hispanics," Pew Research Center report, July 26, 2011, http://www .pewresearch.org/fact-tank/2014/12/12/racial-wealth-gaps -great-recession and http://www.pewsocialtrends.org/2011/07 /26/wealth-gaps-rise-to-record-highs-between-whites-blacks -hispanics.

28. Rakesh Kochhar and Richard Fry, "Wealth inequality has widened along racial, ethnic lines since end of Great Recession," Pew Research Center report, December 12, 2014.

29. Sarah Burd-Sharps and Rebecca Rasch, "Impact of the US Housing Crisis on the Racial Wealth Gap Across Generations," Social Science Research Council, June 2015.

30. Hall, Crowder, and Spring, p. 543.

31. Wes Rivers. "Going, Going, Gone: D.C.'s Affordable Housing Crisis," D.C. Fiscal Policy Institute report, March 12, 2015.

32. Sean Reardon and Kendra Bischoff, "The Continuing Increase in Income Segregation, 2007–2012," Stanford Center for Education Policy Analysis report, March 6, 2016.

33. John R. Logan, "Separate and Unequal in Suburbia," US2010 Project Report (December 1, 2014): 5.

34. Logan, "Separate and Unequal in Suburbia," p. 4.

35. Ibid.

36. Logan, "Separate and Unequal in Suburbia," p. 6.

37. Jamala Rogers, *Ferguson Is America: Roots of Rebellion* (Mira Digital, 2015): 14.

38. Rogers, pp. 19–20.

39. Richard Rothstein, *The Making of Ferguson: Public Policies At The Root of Its Troubles*, Economic Policy Institute report, 2014, http://www.epi.org/publication/making-ferguson.

40. Gordon, p. 213.

41. Jargowsky, p. 14.

42. Douglas S. Massey and Jonathan Tannen, "A Research Note on Trends in Black Hypersegregation," *Demography* 52 (2015): 1028.

HANDS UP: ON FERGUSON

1. Michael Brown Sr., "Read Michael Brown Sr.'s Emotional Father's Day Letter," Esquire.com, June 21, 2015, http://www.esquire.com/news-politics/a35864/read-michael-brown-srs-emotional-fathers-day-letter.

2. Julia Lurie, "10 Hours in Ferguson: A Visual Timeline Of Michael Brown's Death And Its Aftermath," *Mother Jones,* August 27, 2014, http://www.motherjones.com/politics/2014/08/timeline-michael-brown-shooting-ferguson. Brittany Noble reported for KMOV; the video is viewable at https://www.youtube.com/watch?v=K8Lsn8xVc5U.

3. "The Lenco BearCat," http://www.lencoarmor.com/law-enforcement, accessed October 6, 2015. Mark Schlueb, "Orlando Police Shopping for New Armored Vehicle," *Orlando*

Sentinel, September 5, 2014, http://www.orlandosentinel.com
/news/breaking-news/os-orlando-police-armored-car
-20140905-story.html.

4. Mark Follman, "Michael Brown's Mom Laid Flowers
Where He Was Shot—and Police Crushed Them," *Mother
Jones*, August 27, 2014, http://www.motherjones.com/politics
/2014/08/ferguson-st-louis-police-tactics-dogs-michael
-brown.

See also: Julia Lurie, "10 Hours in Ferguson: A Visual
Timeline of Michael Brown's Death and Its Aftermath," *Mother
Jones*, August 27, 2014, http://www.motherjones.com/politics
/2014/08/timeline-michael-brown-shooting-ferguson.

5. Ruth Gilmore, *Golden Gulag: Prisons, Surplus, Crisis,
and Opposition in Globalizing California* (Berkeley: University
of California Press, 2007): 28. "Racism, specifically, is the state-
sanctioned or extralegal production and exploitation of group-
differentiated vulnerability to premature death."

6. Thomas Harvey, John McAnnar, Michael-John Voss,
Megan Conn, Sean Janda, and Sophia Keskey, "Arch City Defenders Municipal Courts White Paper" (Self-published, 2014):
31–32.

7. Radley Balko, "How municipalities In St. Louis County,
Mo., profit from poverty," *Washington Post*, September 3,
2014, https://www.washingtonpost.com/news/the-watch/wp
/2014/09/03/how-st-louis-county-missouri-profits-from
-poverty.

8. United States Department of Justice, Civil Rights Division, "Investigation of the Ferguson Police Department"
(March 4, 2015): 4.

9. Ibid., p. 2.

10. Ibid., pp. 2–3.

11. Michael Daly, "The Day Ferguson Cops Were Caught
in a Bloody Lie," *Daily Beast*, August 15, 2014, http://www
.thedailybeast.com/articles/2014/08/15/the-day-ferguson-cops
-were-caught-in-a-bloody-lie.html.

12. Nicholas Pistor, "St. Louis prosecutor has faced controversy for decades," *St. Louis Post-Dispatch*, August 14, 2014.

13. Michael Petrilli, "The fastest-gentrifying neighborhoods

in the United States," The Thomas B. Fordham Institute, June 11, 2012, http://edexcellence.net/commentary/education-gadfly -daily/flypaper/2012/the-fastest-gentrifying-neighborhoods-in -the-united-states.html.

14. LAPD officer Daryl Gates, later the police chief in charge during the 1992 Los Angeles riots, created SWAT teams in part because of his concern over the police's inability to control Blacks during the 1965 Watts uprising. In December 1969, he debuted the SWAT team with a brutal raid on the Black Panther Party's Los Angeles headquarters. For more on Gates, see *Can't Stop Won't Stop*. For more on the history of SWAT and the militarization of the police, read Radley Balko's invaluable book, *The Rise of the Warrior Cop* (New York: Public Affairs, 2013).

15. Wesley Lowery, "The QuikTrip gas station, Ferguson protestors' staging ground, is now silent," *Washington Post*, August 19, 2014, http://www.washingtonpost.com/politics /ferguson-protesters-staging-ground-the-quiktrip-gas-station -is-now-silent/2014/08/19/a8e4382e-27db-11e4-958c-268a320a60ce _story.html.

16. "The Story Behind an Iconic Photo from Ferguson, Missouri," *Reliable Sources*, August 24, 2014, http://reliablesources .blogs.cnn.com/2014/08/24/web-exclusive-story-behind-iconic -ferguson-photo.

17. Diana Scholl, "Ferguson Q&A with Organizer Larry Fellows III," ACLU, November 23, 2014, https://www.aclu.org /blog/speakeasy/ferguson-qa-organizer-larry-fellows-iii.

18. Wesley Lowery, *Ferguson: Three Minutes that Changed America* (New York: Diversion Books, 2015): 45.

19. "Cops Or Soldiers? Pentagon, DHS Helped Arm Police in Ferguson with Equipment Used in War," *Democracy Now!*, August 15, 2014, http://www.democracynow.org/2014/8/15/cops _or_soldiers_pentagon_dhs_helped.

20. Tef Poe, "Dear Mr. President," *Riverfront Times*, December 1, 2015, http://blogs.riverfronttimes.com/rftmusic/2014 /12/dear_mr_president_a_letter_from_tef_poe.php.

21. Paul Hitlin and Nancy Vogt, "Cable, Twitter picked up Ferguson at a similar clip," Pew Research Center, August 20,

2014, http://www.pewresearch.org/fact-tank/2014/08/20/cable -twitter-picked-up-ferguson-story-at-a-similar-clip.

22. Randall Kennedy, "Lifting As We Climb," *Harper's Magazine* (October 2015): 26.

23. Alicia Garza, "A Herstory of the #BlackLivesMatter Movement," *Feminist Wire*, October 7, 2014, http://www .thefeministwire.com/2014/10/blacklivesmatter-2.

24. Ibid.

25. Nicholas Phillips, "Why Did This 21-Year-Old Woman Die in the Pagedale Jail?" *Riverfront Times*, July 2, 2015, http:// www.riverfronttimes.com/newsblog/2015/07/02/why-did-this -21-year-old-woman-die-in-the-pagedale-jail.

26. "Ferguson October: Youth Organizers Plan Weekend Of Resistance 2 Months After Death of Michael Brown," *Democracy Now!*, October 7, 2014, http://www.democracynow.org /blog/2014/10/7/ferguson_october_youth_organizers_plan _weekend.

27. They marched under the "Moral Monday" banner, a campaign begun by activists in North Carolina fighting for voting rights and racial justice.

28. Koran Addo, "Negotiations, concessions led to end of Occupy SLU," *St. Louis Post-Dispatch*, October 21, 2014, http:// www.stltoday.com/news/local/education/negotiations -concessions-led-to-end-of-occupy-slu-protest/article _7dda5d3e-519b-5ae6-a481-301e1d2dab28.html.

29. Elizabeth Vega said the song choice had been inspired by Rebel Diaz's remixed version of the folk standard, which was popularized by Pete Seeger and became a civil rights movement standard.

30. Nadine Bloch, "The Art of #BlackLivesMatter," *Waging Nonviolence*, January 8, 2015, http://wagingnonviolence.org /feature/art-blacklivesmatter.

31. Rebecca Rivas, "Protestors demonstrate with mass 'die-in' near Delmar and Skinker," *St. Louis American*, November 16, 2014, http://www.stlamerican.com/news/local_news /article_49f76b80-6dcf-11e4-a569-2babf8ed158a.html.

32. *For the Sake of All: A report on the health and well-being of African Americans in St. Louis and why it matters for every-*

one (Washington University in St. Louis and St. Louis University, 2014): 29. Available at: https://forthesakeofall.files.wordpress.com/2014/05/for-the-sake-of-all-report.pdf.

33. You can see these posted at Damon Davis's website at http://heartacheandpaint.com and at http://wailingwallstl.tumblr.com.

34. Nancy Stiles, "MoKaBe's Slammed By CopTalk Message Board for Serving as 'Safe Space' for Protestors," *Riverfront Times,* November 14, 2014, http://www.riverfronttimes.com/foodblog/2014/11/14/mokabes-slammed-by-coptalk-message-board-for-serving-as-safe-space-for-protesters.

35. John Ziegler, UStream video, posted by "Rebelutionary_Z LIVE," November 24, 2014, http://www.ustream.tv/recorded/55806850.

Sara Vipond Brink, "Police Civil Misconduct in Ferguson & St. Louis Vol. 1," Storify, November 24–25, 2014, https://storify.com/Vipondalicious/ferguson-police-civil-misconduct.

36. Matt Pearce, "'Ferguson October' rally highlights divide among St. Louis activists," *Los Angeles Times,* October 12, 2014, http://www.latimes.com/nation/la-na-ferguson-october-debate-20141012-story.html.

Chris McGreal, "St. Louis protests: Ferguson activists reject religious leaders' platitudes," *Guardian,* October 13, 2014, http://www.theguardian.com/us-news/2014/oct/13/st-louis-protests-religious-leaders-messages-anger-ferguson-activists.

37. Reverend Osagyefo Sekou, "The clergy's place is with the protesters in Ferguson," *Al-Jazeera America,* November 23, 2014, http://america.aljazeera.com/opinions/2014/11/ferguson-protestmovementreligious.html.

38. "The Heartbeat of Democracy—Ferguson," YouTube video, 3:58, posted by "Shazza Razza," November 26, 2014, https://www.youtube.com/watch?v=uf-z9zbeRys.

39. Arlene Eisen, "What If Michael Brown Had Been Armed?" Counterpunch.com, September 5, 2014, http://www.counterpunch.org/2014/09/05/what-if-michael-brown-had-been-armed/?utm_source=rss&utm_medium=rss&utm_campaign=what-if-michael-brown-had-been-armed.

Every 28 Hours: Operation Ghetto Storm, November 2014,

http://www.operationghettostorm.org/uploads/1/9/1/1/19110795 /new_all_14_11_04.pdf.

40. "'This Country Values Property over People': Ferguson Activist Speaks Out as Protests Spread," *Democracy Now!*, November 26, 2014, http://www.democracynow.org/2014/11/26 /this_country_values_property_over_people.

41. Chris Hedges, "Rise Of The New Black Radicals," Truth-dig.com, April 26, 2015, http://www.truthdig.com/report/print /rise_of_the_new_black_radicals_20150426

42. Speri, ibid.

43. Lowery, *Ferguson*, 16.

44. Ibid.

45. Trymaine Lee, "Eyewitness to Michael Brown shooting recounts his friend's death," MSNBC.com, August 12, 2014, http://www.msnbc.com/msnbc/eyewitness-michael-brown -fatal-shooting-missouri.

46. Wesley Lowery and Darryl Fears, "Michael Brown and Dorian Johnson, the friend who witnessed his shooting," *Washington Post*, August 31, 2013, https://www.washingtonpost .com/politics/michael-brown-and-dorian-johnson-the-friend -who-witnessed-his-shooting/2014/08/31/bb9b47ba-2ee2-11e4 -9b98-848790384093_story.html.

47. "Department of Justice Report Regarding The Criminal Investigation into the Shooting Death of Michael Brown By Ferguson, Missouri Police Officer Darren Wilson," U.S. De-partment of Justice (March 4, 2015): 74.

48. Nikole Hannah-Jones, "School Segregation, the Con-tinuing Tragedy of Ferguson," *ProPublica*, December 19, 2014, http://www.propublica.org/article/ferguson-school-segregation.

Listen also to Nikole Hannah-Jones, "562: The Problem We All Live With," *This American Life*, NPR, July 31, 2015, http:// www.thisamericanlife.org/radio-archives/episode/562/the -problem-we-all-live-with.

49. Hannah-Jones, "School Segregation." The document referenced can be viewed at https://assets.documentcloud.org /documents/1382594/vatterott-harkin.pdf.

50. Chris Oberholtz, Amy Anderson, and DeAnn Smith,

"Vatterott College told to pay Belton woman $13 million," KCTV 5 News, June 19, 2013, http://www.kctv5.com/story/22634184 /vatterott-college-told-to-pay-belton-woman-13-million. A judge later reduced the damage award to $2 million. But the verdict against Vatterott was affirmed on appeal: http://www.career collegecentral.com/news/appeals-court-upholds-student %E2%80%99s-case-against-vatterott-college.

51. Michael Brown Sr., "Read Michael Brown Sr.'s Emotional Father's Day Letter," *Esquire,* June 21, 2015, http://www .esquire.com/news-politics/a35864/read-michael-brown-srs -emotional-fathers-day-letter.

52. Daniel Bates, "'If I leave this earth today, at least you'll know I care about others more than my damn self': Haunting Facebook message of 'big teddy bear' Michael Brown just days before he was shot dead by cop," *Daily Mail,* August 13, 2014, http://www.dailymail.co.uk/news/article-2723299/If-I-leave -earth-today-youll-know-I-care-damn-self-The-haunting -Facebook-message-gentle-giant-teen-days-shot-cop-sparking -St-Louis-riots.html.

53. "Department of Justice Report Regarding the Criminal Investigation into the Shooting Death of Michael Brown," 29.

54. Lowery, *Ferguson,* 14.

Jeremy Kohler and Robert Patrick, "Workers who were witnesses provide new perspective on Michael Brown shooting," *St. Louis Post-Dispatch,* September 7, 2014, http://www.stltoday .com/news/local/crime-and-courts/workers-who-were -witnesses-provide-new-perspective-on-michael-brown /article_14a3e5f8-6c6a-5deb-92fe-87fcee622c29.html

Shirley Washington, "Exclusive: Witness claims he saw Michael Brown being shot," Fox2Now, August 12, 2014, http:// fox2now.com/2014/08/12/witness-claims-he-saw-what -happened-when-michael-brown-was-shot.

55. "Department of Justice Report Regarding the Criminal Investigation into the Shooting Death of Michael Brown," 37–38.

56. Ibid., 43.

THE IN-BETWEENS: ON ASIAN AMERICANNESS

1. Governor George Ariyoshi, "State of the State Address," January 21, 1980.

2. In California and Michigan, Asian Americans have opposed anti-affirmative action ballot measures by huge proportions. National surveys beginning in 2000 have shown over 60% of Asian Americans support affirmative action, and these surveys have proven remarkably consistent over time and across different Asian American ethnicities. See the following:

Karthick Ramakrishnan, "An Agenda for Justice: Contours of Public Opinion Among Asian Americans," APIA Vote and Asian Americans Advancing Justice Report, November 7, 2014, http://www.apiavote.org/sites/default/files/APV-AAJC-issues -nov7.pdf.

Karthick Ramakrishnan, "California needs to look again at Asian stance on affirmative action," *Los Angeles Times*, September 25, 2014, http://www.latimes.com/opinion/op-ed/la-oe -0925-ramakrishnan-affirmative-action-asians--20140925 -story.html.

Robert Teranishi, "The Attitudes of Asian Americans Toward Affirmative Action," National Commission on Asian American and Pacific Islander Research in Education, 2012, http://care.gseis .ucla.edu/wp-content/uploads/2015/08/CARE-affirmative _action_polling-1v2.pdf National Asian American Survey http:// www.naasurvey.com/reports/affirmative-action.html.

3. See Thomas J. Espenshade and Alexandria Walton Radford, *No Longer Separate, Not Yet Equal: Race and Class in Elite College Admissions and Campus Life.* (Princeton University Press, 2009).

4. Long T. Bui, "A Better Life? Asian Americans and the Necropolitics of Higher Education," *Critical Ethnic Studies: A Reader*, ed. Critical Ethnic Studies Editorial Collective (Durham, NC: Duke University Press, 2016), pp. 161, 171–2.

5. J. Weston Phippen, "Why Was Officer Peter Liang Convicted?" TheAtlantic.com, March 3, 2016, http://www.theatlantic .com/national/archive/2016/03/peter-liang-police-shooting /471687.

Jamiles Lartey, "NYPD officer breaks down during testimony about Akai Gurley shooting," TheGuardian.com, February 8, 2016, http://www.theguardian.com/us-news/2016/feb/08/nypd-officer-peter-liang-testifies-akai-gurley.

CONCLUSION: MAKING LEMONADE

1. Nicholas Mirzoeff, *The Right To Look: A Counterhistory of Visuality* (Durham, NC: Duke University Press, 2011): 1.

2. Beyoncé's take on the Kübler-Ross model of mourning draws from poet and collaborator Warsan Shire's album *warsan versus melancholy (the seven stages of being lonely),* and expands to eleven stages. Bey symbolists haven't missed this: together, the two meet in the track "7/11."

3. Joan Morgan, "Beyoncé, Black Feminist Art And This Oshun Bidness," Genius.com, April 30, 2016, http://genius.com/a/beyonce-black-feminist-art-and-this-oshun-bidness.

4. For music nerds like me, there is a book to be written about Beyoncé and her musical collaborators' careful editing and curation of samples alone. To wit: the strings from Andy Williams's "Can't Get Used to Losing You" and Isaac Hayes's epic orchestral arrangements on Burt Bacharach's "Walk On By" are not just foundational musical elements, they extend the emotion and the ambition of the album. The original songs convey an overwhelming feeling of loss. And Beyoncé's choice to use them signals that she wants her *versions*—let's think dub history and genealogy here—of these songs to be considered on the same level of canonization as the others that have come before. The thwomping, echoing sound of John Bonham's snare on Led Zeppelin's cover of "When the Levee Breaks" amp the chorus of "Don't Hurt Yourself" to the next level, but they also summon a line of allusions that begin in 2005 New Orleans and move back through Mississippi and Louisiana and the blues sung about the destructive powers of river waters breaking their containers (Oshun, again). . . . And, you know I'm just getting warm. . . .

5. Melissa Harris-Perry, "A Call and Response with Melissa Harris-Perry: The Pain and Power of *Lemonade*," *Elle,* April 26,

2016, http://www.elle.com/culture/music/a35903/lemonade-call -and-response.

6. Grace Lee Boggs, *The Next American Revolution* (Berkeley: University of California Press, 2011): xvi.

7. Carrie Mae Weems, Artist statement for "Grace Notes: Reflections For Now," Performance June 4–5, 2016, at Spoleto Festival, College of Charleston. Available at: https://spoletousa .org/events/grace-notes-reflections-for-now.

8. Melissa Harris-Perry, "A Call and Response with Melissa Harris-Perry."

9. Robin D. G. Kelley, "Black Study, Black Struggle: Opening The Debate," *Boston Review,* March 7, 2016, https:// bostonreview.net/forum/robin-d-g-kelley-black-study-black -struggle.

ACKNOWLEDGMENTS

The nation is much different than it was two years ago, when *Who We Be* first came into the world. History hit an inflection point in November 2014, and this book is intended as a response. Although it builds upon *Who We Be*'s foundations, *We Gon' Be Alright* necessarily feels more direct, urgent, and polemical.

Epochs of intense change help clarify our work and direction. For me, that is what the past two years have been about. Personal events have deeply affected me. But we have all seen too how artists have reacted to these serious times by producing brilliant work.

If you've read this far, you already have an idea of some of the music that inspired me as I wrote this book. I have also been moved deeply by the writing of Claudia Rankine, Kiese Laymon, and Ta-Nehisi Coates, the reporting of Nikole Hannah-Jones, Steven Thrasher, and Wesley Lowery, the art of Carrie Mae Weems, B+, Kara Walker, Firelei Baez, Damon Davis, and Favianna Rodriguez, the scholarship of Robin D. G. Kelley, Holly Sidford, and Ruth Gilmore, and the cultural practices of Roberta Uno, Marc Bamuthi Joseph, Dudley Cocke, Jose Antonio Vargas, and Liz Medicine Crow.

As we all are, I am indebted to the young organizers of these surging justice movements. The organizing practices of Opal Tometi, Patrisse Cullors, Alicia Garza, Umi Selah, Aja Monet, Darnell Moore, Karlos Garcia, the DREAMERs, and so many more who have time and again put their bodies on the line have changed our world.

From Ferguson to Earth City, I was privileged to roll with

Malcolm Lizzappi, Tulio Ospina, and Katina Parker. As soon as we hit St. Louis, the Reverend Osagyefo Sekou took us under his wing. Deep gratitude to Bree Newsome, Dr. Cornel West, Pastor André Johnson, Mo Costello and the MoKaBe family, Tef Poe, Ashley Yates, Larry Fellows III, Bukky Gbádégeşin, Brendan Roediger, Rahiel Tesfamariam, Pastor Renita Lamkin, Brittany Ferrell, Alexis Templeton, Keiller MacDuff, Sabaah Jordan, Rosa Clemente, Elizabeth Vega, Montague Simmons, Luke Nephew and the Peace Poets, Patience Zalanga, Jamala Rogers, and Matt Nelson.

I am also thankful to colleagues who have taken me in and pushed me further, whether they intended to or not, whether they knew it or not. In no particular order, they include the irrepressible H. Samy Alim, A-lan Holt, Ellen Oh, Cheryl Brown, Jessica Anderson, Kareem Alston, Miranda Shepherd, Harry and Michele Elam, Kathy Coll, Jennifer Brody, Wayne Au, Mira Shimabukuro, Scott Kurashige, Emily Lawsin, Invincible, Complex Movements, dream hampton, Mike De La Rocha, Greg Tate, Ferentz Lafargue, Christian Frock, Anne Pasternak, Elizabeth and Johan Sorenson, Connie Wolf, Kate Mendillo, Jonathan Calm, Adam Banks, Deborah Cullinan, Maori Karmael Holmes, Rinku Sen, Davey D, W. Kamau Bell, Hari Kondabolu, Nato Green, Moshe Kasher, Jeff Perlstein, Joey Reyes, Alex Soto, Joanne Rondilla, Sarah Burke, Kai Ma, Traci Curry, Victoria Asbury, Michelle Cumbo, Melissa Harris-Perry, Jelani Cobb, Mari Robles, Chinaka Hodge, Elizabeth Alexander, Clyde Valentin, Carlton Turner, Rubén Martínez, Evelyn McDonnell, Amer Ahmed, Min Hyoung Song, Scott Nakagawa, Soya Jung, Caron Atlas, Amita Manghnani, Na'ilah Suad-Nasir, Leigh Raiford, Anna Holmes, john a. powell, Adisa Banjoko, Roberto Gutierrez Varea, Gary Colmenar, Sherise Kimura, Genevieve Leung, Lok Siu, Catherine Ceniza-Choy, Betsy Richards, Eric Liu, Jesse Thorn, Sylvia Chan-Malik, Christina Zanfagna, Loren Kajikawa, Karen L. Ishizuka, Tia Oso, Lori Pourier, Danielle Larsen, Harry Allen, Zaveeni Khan-Marcus, George Lipsitz, Julia Sullivan, Ebrahim Rasool, Rolf Meyer, Tim Phillips, Cat Levin, Cari Levison, Shira Abramowitz, Dave Twombly, James Braxton Peterson, Mike McCormick, Elizabeth Travelslight, Greg Schick, Brad Johnson, Daniel Levin-Becker, the entire staff at Pegasus Books,

Siouxsie Oki, Yo Ann Martinez, Dereca Blackmon, Christine Anagnos, Thelma Golden, Alexis Frasz, David Henry Hwang, Kay WalkingStick, Jamilah King, and Joan Morgan.

I am grateful for the patience, hard work, joy, and humor of my staff and community at Institute for Diversity in the Arts past and present, for my comrades-in-arms Jerome Reyes and Atheel El-Malik, for my teaching assistants Natasha Mmonatau, Yinshi Lerman-Tan, Vivian Lu, Katharine Schwab, Bojan Srbinovski, Casey Wong, and for all of my TAs and students past and present. I am inspired by the Stanford Who's Teaching Us Coalition. Over the years at Stanford, I feel like I'm the one who has been taught and mentored.

For over a decade, I took what amounted to a master class in cultural equity through Roberta Uno's invitation to be part of the Future Aesthetics cohort. I have lots of love for my fellow mentees—Kristen Calhoun, Clyde Valentin, Carlton Turner, Rennie Harris, Steven Sapp, Mildred Ruiz, James Kass, Beth Boone, and Sylvia Sherman. We continued the cycle this past year with the Future Aesthetics documentation team—thank you to Jakeya Caruthers, K.K. Aoki Izu, and all of the super-researchers. I'm also grateful to Jakeya for all the tutoring. Thank you to the Surdna Foundation and the Ford Foundation for the generous support. Big love always to the CultureStr/ke crew, the Culture Group alums, the ArtChangeUS staff, MMAP, EPAA, and my Lavin family, you all give me life.

I'm deeply grateful to the close friends and mentors who read this book in parts or as a whole: Hua Hsu, Ken Chen, Adam Mansbach, Elizabeth Mendez Berry, Oliver Wang, Davey D, Brian Cross, Mari Matsuda, Charles Lawrence, and Gary Delgado. All the failures of the text are entirely my own.

To Stephen Morrison, who saw a book in all of this, Monique Patterson, who helped me find a new voice in the decade after *Can't Stop Won't Stop*, and the entire Picador/Macmillan fam, including Declan Taintor, James Meader, Henry Sene Yee, Kolt Beringer, Shannon Donnelly, Alex Sehulster, and especially Anna deVries, who pushed me further than I thought I could go with humor, brilliance, and grace. Thanks also to Henry Kaufman and Joel Breuklander for all your work.

To Victoria Sanders, Bernadette Baker-Baughman, and the entire crew at VSA for everything always.

An endless food-and-drink tab for my home team: Cody Laux, Lan Anh Le, Debra Pacio, and Alexis Wood for research and media; Hassan Rahim and Jon-Kyle Mohr for the websites; Stephen Serrato for the design wisdom; and Gabrielle Zucker for MVP awesomeness.

To my family, as long as I have breath, it is keyed to the rhythm of you.

~J
Berkeley, CA
May 2016

ABOUT THE AUTHOR

JEFF CHANG is the author of *Can't Stop Won't Stop: A History of the Hip-Hop Generation* and *Who We Be: The Colorization of America* (published in paperback *as Who We Be: A Cultural History of Race in Post–Civil Rights America*). He has been a USA Ford Fellow in Literature and the winner of the American Book Award and the Asian American Literary Award. He is the executive director of the Institute for Diversity in the Arts at Stanford University.